REFLECT

READING & WRITING

LAURIE BLASS

MARI VARGO

**NATIONAL
GEOGRAPHIC
LEARNING**

Australia · Brazil · Mexico · Singapore · United Kingdom · United States

National Geographic Learning,
a Cengage Company

Reflect 3 Reading & Writing
Authors: Laurie Blass & Mari Vargo

Publisher: Sherrise Roehr
Executive Editor: Laura Le Dréan
Senior Development Editor: Eve Einselen Yu
Director of Global Marketing: Ian Martin
Product Marketing Manager: Tracy Baillie
Senior Content Project Manager: Mark Rzeszutek
Media Researcher: Stephanie Eenigenburg
Art Director: Brenda Carmichael
Senior Designer: Lisa Trager
Operations Coordinator: Hayley Chwazik-Gee
Manufacturing Buyer: Mary Beth Hennebury
Composition: MPS Limited

For permission to use material from this text or product,
submit all requests online at **cengage.com/permissions**
Further permissions questions can be emailed to
permissionrequest@cengage.com

Student Book ISBN: 978-0-357-44850-2
Student Book with Online Practice: 978-0-357-44856-4

National Geographic Learning
200 Pier 4 Boulevard
Boston, MA 02210

Locate your local office at **international.cengage.com/region**

Visit National Geographic Learning online at **ELTNGL.com**
Visit our corporate website at **www.cengage.com**

Printed in China
Print Number: 01   Print Year: 2021

SCOPE AND SEQUENCE

WRITING	GRAMMAR	CRITICAL THINKING	REFLECT ACTIVITIES
Organize a paragraph	Multi-word verbs	Support your opinion	▶ Discuss reasons for having a strong community ▶ Assess ways to meet people ▶ Evaluate a neighborhood ▶ Apply ideas to your neighborhood ▶ **UNIT TASK** Write a paragraph about your ideal community
Write a topic sentence	Simple past and past continuous	Personalize new information	▶ Brainstorm ways we communicate ▶ Analyze your body language ▶ Identify ways that language changes ▶ Predict how English will evolve ▶ **UNIT TASK** Write a narrative paragraph about a cultural misunderstanding
Write supporting ideas and details	Adjective clauses	Synthesize information	▶ Assess why we do things that cause fear ▶ Understand fear in your life ▶ Rank situations that cause fear ▶ Synthesize information from the readings ▶ **UNIT TASK** Write a movie review
Summarize charts and graphs	Simple past and present perfect	Assess features to form an opinion	▶ Match skills to STEM jobs ▶ Evaluate STEAM careers ▶ Compare humans with technology ▶ Assess robot art ▶ **UNIT TASK** Write a paragraph about a graph

WRITING	GRAMMAR	CRITICAL THINKING	REFLECT ACTIVITIES
Write a concluding sentence	Connecting words for reasons and results	Evaluate ideas	▶ Consider reasons to travel ▶ Describe types of vacations ▶ Evaluate vacation activities ▶ Plan an experiential trip in your town ▶ **UNIT TASK** Write an expository paragraph about a trip
Expand a paragraph into an essay	Modals of possibility	Analyze pros and cons	▶ Analyze why we dream ▶ Assess research on dreams ▶ Consider the meaning of dreams ▶ Respond to the idea of recording dreams ▶ **UNIT TASK** Write an essay about the pros and cons of recording dreams
Write an introductory paragraph	Verbs followed by gerunds or infinitives	Question sources	▶ Identify creative companies ▶ Evaluate creative behaviors ▶ Brainstorm ways to be more creative ▶ Apply tips to be creative ▶ **UNIT TASK** Write an essay about how to solve a problem creatively
Write a concluding paragraph	Adverb clauses of contrast	Evaluate the practicality of advice	▶ Assess technology for young learners ▶ Relate ideas to your education ▶ Consider technology for learning new information ▶ Evaluate tech learning tips ▶ **UNIT TASK** Write an opinion essay about ed tech

CONNECT TO IDEAS

Reflect Reading & Writing features relevant, global content to engage students while helping them acquire the academic language and skills they need. Specially-designed activities give students the opportunity to reflect on and connect ideas and language to their academic, work, and personal lives.

Academic, real-world passages invite students to explore the world while building reading skills and providing ideas for writing.

Each unit starts with a **high-interest video** to introduce the theme and generate pre-reading discussion.

CONNECT TO ACADEMIC SKILLS

Focused **reading skills** help create confident academic readers.

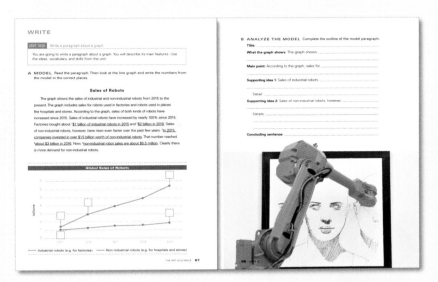

Reflect activities give students opportunities to think critically about what they are learning and check their understanding.

Clear writing models and **Analyze the model** activities give students a strong framework to improve their writing.

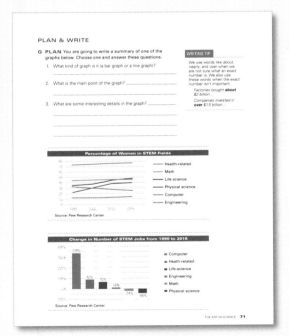

GRAMMAR Simple past and present perfect

We use the **simple past** to describe an event or time period that is completed.

*Between 2005 and 2018, STEM jobs **grew** from about 6.4 million to almost 8 million.*

*Jobs in computer science **increased** 100 percent last year.*

We use the **present perfect** to talk about things that started in the past and continue today.

*STEM jobs **have grown** steadily for the past several years.*

*Jobs in computer science **have increased** almost 100 percent each year since 2011.*

To form the present perfect, use *have* or *has (not)* + the past participle of a verb.

*Sales **have remained** the same for the past five years. They **have not risen**.*

*The rate **has risen** and **fallen** several times since 2016.*

We often use these time words and phrases with the present perfect:

for several years   since 2000   over the years   lately   already   yet

A **step-by-step approach** to the **writing process** along with relevant grammar helps students complete the final writing task with confidence.

CONNECT TO ACHIEVEMENT

Reflect at the end of the unit is an opportunity for formative assessment. Students review the skills and vocabulary they have gained.

DIGITAL RESOURCES

TEACH lively, engaging lessons that get students to participate actively. The Classroom Presentation Tool helps teachers to present the Student's Book pages, play audio and video, and increase participation by providing a central focus for the class.

LEARN AND TRACK with Online Practice and Student's eBook. For students, the mobile-friendly platform optimizes learning through customized re-teaching and adaptive practice. For instructors, progress-tracking is made easy through the shared gradebook.

ASSESS learner performance and progress with the ExamView® Assessment Suite. For assessment, teachers create and customize tests and quizzes easily using the ExamView® Assessment Suite, available online.

ACKNOWLEDGMENTS

The Authors and Publisher would like to acknowledge the teachers around the world who participated in the development of *Reflect*.

A special thanks to our Advisory Board for their valuable input during the development of this series.

ADVISORY BOARD

Dr. Mansoor S. Almalki, Taif University, Saudi Arabia; **John Duplice**, Sophia University, Japan; **Heba Elhadary**, Gulf University for Science and Technology, Kuwait; **Hind Elyas**, Niagara College, Saudi Arabia; **Cheryl House**, ILSC Education Group, Canada; **Xiao Luo**, BFUS International, China; **Daniel L. Paller,** Kinjo Gakuin University, Japan; **Ray Purdy**, ELS Education Services, USA; **Sarah Symes,** Cambridge Street Upper School, USA.

GLOBAL REVIEWERS

ASIA

Michael Crawford, Dokkyo University, Japan; **Ronnie Hill**, RMIT University Vietnam, Vietnam; **Aaron Nurse**, Golden Path Academics, Vietnam; **Simon Park**, Zushi Kaisei, Japan; **Aunchana Punnarungsee**, Majeo University, Thailand.

LATIN AMERICA AND THE CARIBBEAN

Leandro Aguiar, inFlux, Brazil; **Sonia Albertazzi-Osorio**, Costa Rica Institute of Technology, Costa Rica; **Auricea Bacelar**, Top Seven Idiomas, Brazil; **Natalia Benavides**, Universidad de Los Andes, Colombia; **James Bonilla**, Global Language Training UK, Colombia; **Diego Bruekers Deschamp**, Inglês Express, Brazil; **Josiane da Rosa**, Hello Idiomas, Brazil; **Marcos de Campos Bueno**, It's Cool International, Brazil; **Sophia De Carvalho**, Ingles Express, Brazil; **André Luiz dos Santos**, IFG, Brazil; **Oscar Gomez-Delgado**, Universidad de los Andes, Colombia; **Ruth Elizabeth Hibas**, Inglês Express, Brazil; **Rebecca Ashley Hibas**, Inglês Express, Brazil; **Cecibel Juliao**, UDELAS University, Panama; **Rosa Awilda López Fernández**, School of Languages UNAPEC University, Dominican Republic; **Isabella Magalhães**, Fluent English Pouso Alegre, Brazil; **Gabrielle Marchetti**, Teacher's House, Brazil; **Sabine Mary**, INTEC, Dominican Republic; **Miryam Morron**, Corporación Universitaria Americana, Colombia; **Mary Ruth Popov**, Ingles Express, Ltda., Brazil; **Leticia Rodrigues Resende**, Brazil; **Margaret Simons**, English Center, Brazil.

MIDDLE EAST

Abubaker Alhitty, University of Bahrain, Bahrain; **Jawaria Iqbal**, Saudi Arabia; **Rana Khan**, Algonquin College, Kuwait; **Mick King**, Community College of Qatar, Qatar; **Seema Jaisimha Terry**, German University of Technology, Oman.

USA AND CANADA

Thomas Becskehazy, Arizona State University, AZ; **Robert Bushong**, University of Delaware, DE; **Ashley Fifer**, Nassau Community College, NY; **Sarah Arva Grosik**, University of Pennsylvania, PA; **Carolyn Ho**, Lone Star College-CyFair, TX; **Zachary Johnsrud**, Norquest College, Canada; **Caitlin King**, IUPUI, IN; **Andrea Murau Haraway**, Global Launch / Arizona State University, AZ; **Bobbi Plante**, Manitoba Institute of Trades and Technology, Canada; **Michael Schwartz**, St. Cloud State University, MN; **Pamela Smart-Smith**, Virginia Tech, VA; **Kelly Smith**, English Language Institute, UCSD Extension, CA; **Karen Vallejo**, University of California, CA.

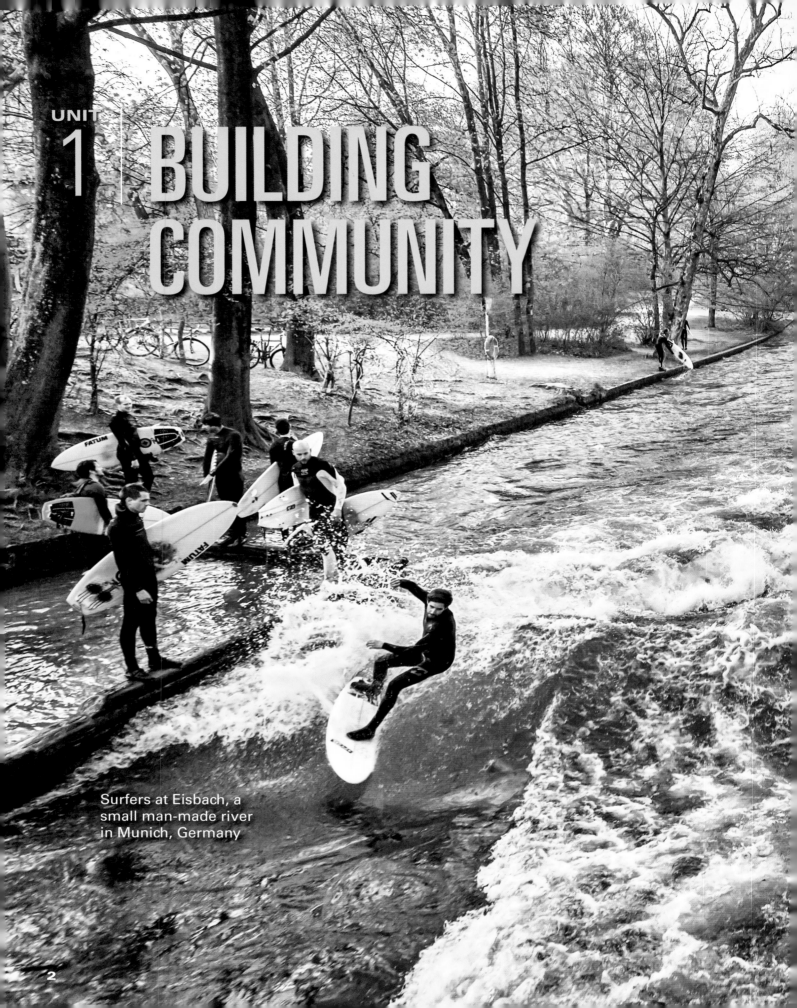

BUILDING COMMUNITY

Surfers at Eisbach, a small man-made river in Munich, Germany

IN THIS UNIT

▶ Discuss reasons for having a strong community

▶ Assess ways to meet people

▶ Evaluate a neighborhood

▶ Apply ideas to your neighborhood

▶ Write a paragraph about your ideal community

SKILLS

READING
Understand main ideas and details

WRITING
Organize a paragraph

GRAMMAR
Multi-word verbs

CRITICAL THINKING
Support your opinion

CONNECT TO THE TOPIC

1. Where are the people in the photo? What are they doing?

2. Who do you think built this space, and why? Explain.

WATCH

Montreal,
Quebec, Canada

WHAT DOES COMMUNITY MEAN TO YOU?

A Watch the video and choose the best answer to complete each statement. ▶ 1.1

1. The people are mostly **teenagers / young adults / middle-aged**.

2. They probably live in a **village / small town / city**.

3. Community is **not very / somewhat / very** important for most of them.

B Watch again. Put the responses in the order that you hear them (2–8). ▶ 1.1

Community is a place…

_____ with like-minded people.

_____ that's walkable.

___1___ where people work together.

_____ where you can sit down.

_____ with restaurants and shops.

_____ where you know everybody.

_____ with a movie theater.

_____ that's peaceful.

CRITICAL THINKING Support your opinion

When you give an opinion, support it with reasons. This will make your opinions more believable.
For example, if you think a community should be walkable, give reasons for that opinion.

I think it's important to have a lot of places you can walk to. This is good for your health because you get exercise. It also reduces pollution from cars and saves you money.

C Read the responses in activity B again. Which features of a community do you think are most important? Tell a partner your ideas. Support your opinion.

PREPARE TO READ

A VOCABULARY Read the definitions. Then complete the sentences with the correct form of the words.

deal with (v phr) to take action on	**impact** (v) to affect
effect (n) a result	**lonely** (adj) having no one to talk to or be with
effort (n) a big push or attempt to do something	**productive** (adj) able to do or achieve a lot
expert (n) someone who is very skilled	**social** (adj) of or about people
human (n) a person	**volunteer** (v) to offer to do something

1. A(n) _____ is someone who knows a lot about a topic or subject.

2. A good way to meet people is through _____ activities like sports and clubs.

3. Some people are _____ in the mornings. Others get work done at night.

4. Making friends can be difficult in a big city, so many people are _____.

5. _____ need to connect with others to be happy and healthy.

6. A park can _____ a community in many positive ways.

7. If you _____ for a charity, you can help people in need.

8. You have to _____ a lot of traffic when you drive in a big city.

9. Online communities have good and bad _____ on people.

10. You must make a(n) _____ to meet people if you move somewhere new.

B PERSONALIZE Discuss these questions with a partner.

1. Why might people feel **lonely** in a big city?
2. What kind of **social** activities do you enjoy?
3. If you had more time to **volunteer**, what type of organization would you work with?

REFLECT Discuss reasons for having a strong community.

Before you read about why we need community, reflect on why community is important. How can a neighborhood or community change people's lives? Write notes about your ideas. Share your ideas in a small group.

_____

_____

_____

_____

READ

WHY WE NEED COMMUNITIES

A PREDICT Check (✓) the reasons for needing community that you think will be in the article.

☐ reduces stress

☐ helps you sleep better

☐ makes you live longer

☐ makes it easier to go out and exercise

☐ stops you from feeling lonely

☐ makes it easier to buy healthy foods

🎧 1.1

1   Most of us like living near other people in a community. Why? Early **humans** lived in large groups called tribes. Tribes were necessary to keep people alive. People in tribes shared food and kept each other safe. As a result, our brains are hardwired[1] to connect with other people. Being part of a community—a modern kind of tribe—**impacts** our health and happiness in many ways.

2   Studies show that people who are less connected to a community are more likely to get sick. A recent survey[2] in the United Kingdom found that nearly ten million people said they often felt **lonely**. That's one in six people in the whole country. In fact, loneliness is increasing around the world. When we are lonely, we feel stressed. Stress can lead to health problems such as heart disease and weight gain, **experts** say.

People relaxing by Cheong-Gyecheon stream in Seoul, Korea

A study in 2013 showed that having few **social** connections is worse for your health than smoking cigarettes.

3   Being in a community has many positive **effects**. If we are sick, close social connections help us get better faster. And they help us sleep better, too. One study showed that being part of a community gives you a 50 percent chance of living longer. People who have good social connections do better at school. They are also more **productive** at work and keep their jobs longer.

4   There are several ways we can get more of the positive effects from our communities. Using Nextdoor, a neighborhood social networking app, is one way. For example, Joan in Barcelona, Spain, used Nextdoor to tell neighbors that he needed help. He wanted to make a movie. Over forty neighbors **volunteered** to help. Joan's neighbors learned new skills while they made a movie together. They became good friends, too. Dr. Emma Seppala of Stanford University studies the effects of social connections. She says there are other ways people can connect in their community. These include getting a pet and meeting other pet owners, or taking a class and learning something new.

5   In conclusion, it might take **effort**, but the benefits of making connections in your community are worth it. Communities make us feel good and help us **deal with** the problem of loneliness. Connect with your community today.

¹**hardwired** (adj) natural way of thinking or behaving
²**survey** (n) a set of questions designed to ask people's opinions

> ## READING SKILL Understand main ideas and details
>
> The **main idea** is the most important idea in a paragraph. It is often stated in the first or second sentence of a paragraph. The main idea guides the rest of the paragraph. **Details** give more information or explain the main idea. Details answer *who, what, when, where, why,* and *how* questions that support the main idea.

B MAIN IDEAS Underline the main ideas in paragraphs 2–4.

C MAIN IDEAS Write the correct paragraph number (2–4) next to its main idea.

a. _____ There are benefits to belonging to a community.

b. _____ Not being part of a community can be unhealthy.

c. _____ There are ways to connect to people in communities.

D DETAILS Write short answers to the questions. Use details from the article.

1. What is a growing problem around the world? _____

2. What causes some people to gain weight or get heart disease? _____

3. When was the study about the effects of social connections published? _____

4. What are four health benefits of being part of a community? _____

_____

_____

5. Where was the neighborhood movie made? _____

6. How did the movie project benefit the neighborhood? _____

_____

REFLECT	Assess ways to meet people.

> **What are the best ways to meet people in your community? Add your own ideas. Check your top three. Then discuss your reasons with a partner.**
>
> ☐ Say "hi" to your neighbors   ☐ Join a social club
>
> ☐ Take your dog for a walk   ☐ Volunteer
>
> ☐ Do a fitness activity or sport   ☐ Communicate through an online app
>
> ☐ _____   ☐ _____

PREPARE TO READ

A VOCABULARY Complete the sentences with the correct form of the words. Use a dictionary if necessary.

central (adj)	design (v)	generation (n)	public (adj)	resident (n)
create (v)	gather (v)	privacy (n)	recommend (v)	style (n)

1. A program helps _____ of San Francisco plant trees in their neighborhoods.

2. The older _____ is less likely to have a community of friends online.

3. One of the nicest _____ places in Seoul is Haneul Park. People go there to walk.

4. The report _____ that the city add more bus stops for people who don't drive.

5. People often _____ at this café. It's a good place to meet friends.

6. The _____ meeting place on campus is the fountain. It's in the middle of everything.

7. Some people build fences around their homes because they want _____. Other people think fences make it difficult to get to know neighbors.

8. When architects _____ buildings, they think about how people will use them.

9. There are many ways to _____ a better community. For example, you can have a neighborhood party or start a community garden.

10. Kenzo Takada lives in a typical Japanese-_____ house in Paris.

B PERSONALIZE Discuss these questions with a partner.

1. What **style** of house do you prefer—traditional or modern? Explain.

2. What is a popular **public** space in your town or city? When do people like to **gather** there?

REFLECT   Evaluate a neighborhood.

You are going to read about city design. Before you do, think of a neighborhood you know well. What makes it a good place to live? What is not so good about it? Complete the chart below. Then share your ideas with a classmate.

Good things about the neighborhood	Bad things about the neighborhood

HAPPY CITIES, BY DESIGN

Public green spaces in São
Paolo, Brazil, help residents
to be happy and healthy.

A PREDICT Look at the photo. Read the title and the headings. What do
you think the article is mostly about?

a. Top cities for people to move to

b. Tips on making your community a happier place to live

c. Places where governments have improved communities

1   What makes a city a healthy and happy place to live? Charles Montgomery, founder of Happy City, thinks he knows. Happy City helps cities **design** community spaces so that **residents** can be happier and healthier. Montgomery thinks that social connections are the most important factor in human happiness. His research found that these connections are improved in cities that:

▶ have green spaces
▶ are walkable
▶ are quiet
▶ are safe
▶ and bring people together.

Here are a few examples of government projects that have helped people connect.

CONNECTING NEIGHBORS IN THE UNITED ARAB EMIRATES (UAE)

2   Modern neighborhoods in the UAE have a lot of single-family homes. They also have large front yards. These communities looked nice, but residents were not connecting with their neighbors. Happy City worked with local officials to research the problem. The answer was simple. They **recommended** the UAE look to the past and build traditional houses. In the UAE, many **generations** often live together. It's important that they have a place to meet in the house. However, family members still need **privacy**. A traditional **style** house has a courtyard[1]. Courtyards provide both private spaces and areas for people to come together. Happy City also suggested adding **central** meeting places such as squares[2] to neighborhoods. People can meet each other in these squares when they are out.

TRAIN STATION GARDENING IN TOKYO

3   Officials in Tokyo, Japan, wanted to **create** more green areas in the city. This is difficult because there are so few open spaces in the city. But a railway company had an idea—build community gardens on top of railway stations. These small **public** gardens are for people to grow vegetables on. Residents can rent a space for a year. Experts teach people how to grow plants. Families and train passengers spend time in the gardens getting to know each other. Today, there are five of these railway station gardens in Tokyo. "We're building a community…in which the local residents can take part and have fun," says a spokesperson for the railway company.

A MEETING PLACE IN SÃO PAULO

4   São Paulo is a huge city of more than 12 million people. In 2012, the mayor[3] asked architects to **design** more ways for residents to meet. One simple solution was to change an unused square into a place for residents to **gather**. They added seating under trees. They also added bathrooms and free wi-fi. They put bicycle lanes around the square and made it safer to cross the roads. Now, the square has concerts and an outdoor cinema. As a result, over 200 percent more people use the square now than before.

---

[1]**courtyard** (n) an open area, without a roof, that is enclosed by the walls of a building
[2]**square** (n) an open, public space in city or town
[3]**mayor** (n) the elected leader of a city

B MAIN IDEAS Complete the main ideas. Use one or two words from the article.

Paragraph 1: Improving _____ in cities will help people to be happier.

Paragraph 2: To help residents connect, the UAE plans to return to _____ houses.

Paragraph 3: To create more green space, Tokyo created gardens above _____.

Paragraph 4: To help residents meet each other, São Paulo improved a(n) _____.

C DETAILS Read the statements about Montgomery's research in paragraph 1. Write T for *True*, F for *False*, or NG for *Not Given*.

People are happier in cities…

1. _____ with streets that are car-free.

2. _____ that have places where people can meet.

3. _____ that have no apartment blocks.

4. _____ with parks and gardens.

5. _____ that are noisy.

6. _____ that are not dangerous.

D DETAILS Complete the chart with the correct details (a–h).

The UAE	Tokyo, Japan	São Paulo, Brazil
_____ _____	_____ _____ _____	_____ _____ _____

a. Residents can rent a space.

b. Planners found that traditional houses are better.

c. Planners put in wi-fi.

d. There's a square with places to sit in the shade.

e. Residents meet train passengers.

f. Planners put meeting places in the neighborhoods.

g. Residents learn how to grow plants.

h. A safer way to cross the street is one improvement.

REFLECT Apply ideas to your neighborhood.

Think of a part of your city or town that could be nicer. Which ideas in the article might help improve that part of town? Write your ideas in your notebook. Then share your ideas with a partner.

WRITE

Write a paragraph about your ideal community.

You are going to write a response to a survey asking: "What is your ideal community?" Use the ideas, skills, and vocabulary from the unit.

A MODEL Read the paragraph. Would you like to live in this community? Share your ideas with a partner.

My Ideal Community

My ideal community is a healthy place for residents and for the Earth. First of all, my ideal community is walkable. For example, I want to easily pick up groceries or drop off laundry on foot. Getting around without a car is important to me. This is because fewer cars means better air quality. Secondly, my ideal community is a zero-waste community. Zero-waste means nothing gets thrown away. For example, restaurants and cafes do not throw away unsold food. Finally, my ideal community helps people keep fit. For example, there are a lot of parks and gyms where people can get together and exercise. These places are good for physical and mental health. A place that makes it easy for people and the planet to stay healthy is my idea of a perfect community.

WRITING SKILL Organize a paragraph

A **paragraph** is a group of sentences about one main idea.
- The **topic sentence** introduces the main idea. It is often the first or second sentence.
- **Supporting ideas** are smaller ideas about the topic sentence. There are often two or more supporting ideas in a paragraph.
- **Details** give more information about each supporting idea.
- The **concluding sentence** is the final sentence of the paragraph. It usually restates the topic sentence in different words.

B APPLY Complete the tasks.

1. Underline the topic sentence and the concluding sentence in the model.

2. Check (✓) the three supporting ideas.

C ANALYZE THE MODEL Complete the outline of the model.

Title: My Ideal Community

Topic sentence: My ideal community is _____.

_____

Supporting idea 1: It's walkable.

    Details: can pick up _____ or drop off _____

    fewer cars mean better _____

Supporting idea 2: It's a _____ community.

    Details: means nothing gets _____

    restaurants and cafes don't _____

Supporting idea 3: It helps people _____

    Details: lots of _____ and gyms, and other places good for

    physical and mental health

Concluding sentence: A place that _____

is my idea of a perfect community.

D APPLY Read the sentences below the paragraph. Then complete the paragraph with the correct topic and supporting sentences. Write the letters in the blanks. There is one extra.

How to Meet New People

    ¹_____ First of all, try to get to know your neighbors. ²_____ This way, you meet new people and also learn about the best shops and restaurants. ³_____ Yoga classes, for example, are a great way to make new friends. In these classes you meet people who have a similar interest. Finally, you can volunteer in your community. ⁴_____ Volunteering is a good way to meet people and do good things at the same time. In short, there a lot of ways to improve your life and meet new people at the same time.

    a. For example, you can introduce yourself and ask them for recommendations.

    b. Secondly, you can join a team.

    c. Secondly, you can join a gym or exercise class.

    d. For example, you can help plan and organize neighborhood events.

    e. There are many ways to meet people when you move to a new place.

GRAMMAR Multi-word verbs

Verbs with two or three words are common. They are usually formed with a verb + a preposition or particle. Sometimes the meaning of these multi-word verbs is clear. For example, to *move in* means "to go live in a new home." The meanings of other multi-word verbs are not as obvious. For example, to *pick up* can mean "to get someone or something from another place." It's a good idea to learn these verbs as units. Here are some common multi-word verbs to use when writing about communities:

ask around	get around	meet up with	run into
drop off*	get together	move in*	sign up*
eat out	help out*	pick up*	throw away*
get along with	look forward to	put together*	work out*

*These are **separable verbs**. You can separate some two-word verbs with an object. For example: *You can **pick up** your laundry tomorrow. You can **pick** it **up** after 3 p.m.*

E GRAMMAR Underline the multi-word verbs in the model paragraph in activity A.

F GRAMMAR Read the definitions. Write the correct multi-word verb from the Grammar box. Use a dictionary to help.

1. _____: have dinner at a restaurant

2. _____: meet on purpose

3. _____: meet accidentally

4. _____: exercise

5. _____: get information by talking to people

6. _____: feel happy about a future event

7. _____: leave something somewhere

8. _____: put into the trash

G GRAMMAR Complete the sentences with the correct forms of the multi-word verbs.

ask around	help out	get along with	pick up	run into	sign up

1. If you like to _____, try volunteering.

2. If you want to relax and meet other people, _____ for a yoga class at the gym.

3. The grocery store is a place where you might _____ your neighbors.

4. If you want to _____ your neighbors, be quiet after 11 p.m.

5. It's a good idea to _____ for restaurant recommendations. The locals usually know the best places.

6. Some supermarkets let you order online and _____ your food _____ outside the store.

H GRAMMAR Write sentences about yourself and your community with the verbs.

1. (get along with) _____
2. (run into) _____
3. (get around) _____
4. (look forward to) _____
5. (put up with) _____
6. (eat out) _____
7. (help out) _____
8. (meet up with) _____

I EDIT Read the paragraph. Find and correct five errors with multi-word verbs.

My Ideal Community

My ideal community helps people connect. I live alone, so I want to live in a community where it's easy to meet up people. First of all, I prefer a small community. It's easier to run to people in a small town. For example, in a small town, you often see your friends and neighbors around. You see them when eating up at a restaurant or dropping your laundry up. Second, my ideal community has a lot of public places that are designed for older people. For example, there are parks and squares that have comfortable places to sit. Finally, my ideal community has places that make it easy for people to get up. There are cafés and restaurants that aren't too expensive. There are also events to attend, like outdoor concerts or movies. In conclusion, my ideal community is a place where it's easy to meet people.

The park in the central square (Plaza Mayor) in Antigua, Guatemala

PLAN & WRITE

J BRAINSTORM What is your ideal community like? Complete the concept map with the ideas from the unit or your own ideas.

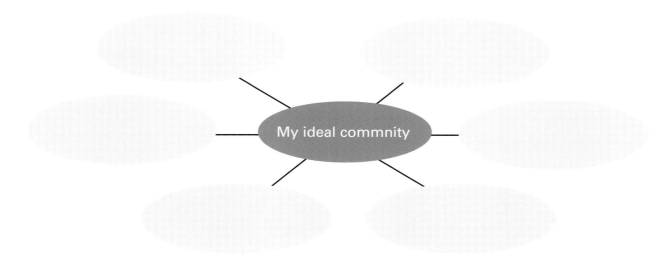

My ideal commnity

K OUTLINE Complete the outline. Choose the three most important ideas from your brainstorming. These are your supporting ideas.

Title: My Ideal Community

Topic sentence: My ideal community _____

Supporting idea 1: _____

Details: _____

_____

Supporting idea 2: _____

Details: _____

_____

Supporting idea 3: _____

Details: _____

_____

Concluding sentence: _____

L FIRST DRAFT Use your outline to write a first draft of your paragraph.

M REVISE Use this list as you write your second draft.

☐ Does your topic sentence include the main idea of your paragraph?

☐ Does your paragraph have two or three supporting ideas?

☐ Does each supporting idea have one or two details?

☐ Does your paragraph have a concluding sentence?

N EDIT Use this list as you write your final draft.

☐ Did you use multi-word verbs correctly?

☐ Do your subjects and verbs agree?

☐ Did you spell all the words correctly?

☐ Did you use correct punctuation?

O FINAL DRAFT Reread your paragraph and correct any errors. Then submit it to your teacher.

Colorful homes in Upernavik, Greenland

REFLECT

A Check (✓) the Reflect activities you can do and the academic skills you can use.

☐ discuss reasons for having a strong community   ☐ understand main ideas and details

☐ assess ways to meet people   ☐ organize a paragraph

☐ evaluate a neighborhood   ☐ multi-word verbs

☐ apply ideas to your neighborhood   ☐ support your opinion

☐ write a paragraph about your ideal community

B Write the vocabulary words from the unit in the correct column. Add any other words that you learned. Circle words you still need to practice.

NOUN	VERB	ADJECTIVE	ADVERB & OTHER

C Reflect on the ideas in the unit as you answer these questions.

1. What information about creating communities did you find the most interesting or useful? Explain.

_____

_____

_____

2. What ideas or skills in this unit will be most useful to you in the future? Explain.

_____

_____

_____

LANGUAGE
ON THE MOVE

An Italian couple in their kitchen

IN THIS UNIT

▶ Brainstorm ways we communicate

▶ Analyze your body language

▶ Identify ways that language changes

▶ Predict how English will evolve

▶ Write a paragraph about a cultural misunderstanding

SKILLS

READING
Understand charts

WRITING
Write a topic sentence

GRAMMAR
Simple past and past continuous

CRITICAL THINKING
Personalize new information

CONNECT TO THE TOPIC

1. What do you think the woman might be trying to communicate?

2. What do you think the title means? What will the unit be about?

The woman from the video discusses her experience with a friend from another culture.

ON NON-VERBAL COMMUNICATION

A **PREDICT** Read the title and the caption. What kind of experience do you think the woman in the photo is discussing? Check your answer after you watch.

B Watch the video. Put the types of non-verbal communication in the order that you hear about them. ▶ 2.1

a._____ making facial expressions

b._____ touching someone gently

c._____ making motions with or moving your hands

d._____ making sounds, such as "hmm"

C Why did the woman have a difficult time with her friend?

a. The sound "hmm" is not used by her friend.

b. The meaning of the sound "hmm" is different for each of them.

c. Her friend did not understand her facial expression.

D What are examples of non-verbal communication in your culture? Are there any that might create a problem with people from other cultures?

PREPARE TO READ

A VOCABULARY Complete the sentences with the correct form of the words. Use a dictionary if necessary.

according to (prep)	emotion (n)	misunderstanding (n)	pay attention (v phr)	similar (adj)
avoid (v)	maintain (v)	necessary (adj)	recognize (v)	uncomfortable (adj)

1. In many cultures, it is polite to _____ eye contact and not look down when speaking to someone.

2. _____ experts, the most widely spoken languages are Chinese, Spanish, and English.

3. Happiness and sadness are _____.

4. It's a good idea to _____ to your teacher when she is explaining English grammar.

5. When you travel to a new place, you may not _____ the different foods in a restaurant.

6. "Happy" or "sad" emojis make messages clearer so there are fewer _____.

7. Speaking in front of large groups of people makes many people feel _____.

8. When you go to a different country, some customs will be _____ to yours while others will be very different.

9. Travelers should _____ using body language that upsets local people.

10. It isn't _____ to learn the language before visiting a country, but it is useful to learn a few phrases before you go.

B PERSONALIZE Discuss these questions with a partner.

1. Think of someone from a different culture. What are some things in their culture that are **similar** to yours? What are some things that are different?

2. What is a good way to **avoid misunderstandings** with people from different cultures?

REFLECT   Brainstorm ways we communicate.

Before you read about how we communicate, answer the questions. Then share your ideas with a partner.

1. What forms of communication do we often use (e.g., texting)?

   _____

2. How do we use our bodies to communicate with each other?

   _____

READ

CAN YOU "READ THE AIR"?

A PREDICT Discuss the questions with a partner.

1. Do you think the people are enjoying the speakers?
2. What do you think the title means?

An audience listens to speakers talking about the power of culture.

🎧 2.1

1   The words we say are important. They tell a listener about our thoughts and **emotions**. But words may not be the most important way to communicate meaning. **According to** one study, only seven percent of meaning comes from words. Instead, meaning comes mostly from non-verbal communication. Non-verbal communication includes your tone of voice[1] and your body language. This non-verbal communication can cause **misunderstandings** when you are talking to someone from a different culture.

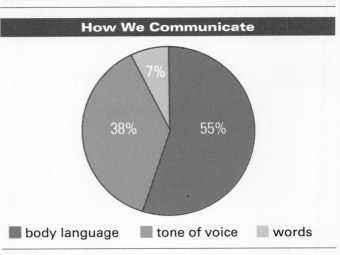

How We Communicate

- 7%
- 38%
- 55%

■ body language   ■ tone of voice   ■ words

2 In Japan, for example, non-verbal communication is very important. Business speaker Erin Meyer gives an example of this. She gave a presentation to a group of people in Japan, and at the end, she asked if anyone had any questions. No one raised their hand, so she sat down. A Japanese colleague[2] told her that he thought some people *did* have questions. She was surprised. So, he asked the group if they had any questions, and again, no one raised their hands. But then he looked closely at the people in the group and asked a woman if she had a question. She did! Afterwards, Meyer asked her colleague how he knew that the woman had a question. He explained that in Japan, people who are looking at you directly often have questions.

3 Meyer's experience shows it is **necessary** to "read the air." Reading the air is based on a Japanese expression. It means to be skilled at **recognizing** people's non-verbal language. In Japan, not being able to "read the air" can ruin business deals and relationships.

COMMENTS

👤 Naveed

4 Interesting article. Thank you! I just learned that English speakers expect people to **maintain** eye contact when they are talking. Yesterday, I was talking to my teacher, and I **avoided** looking into her eyes. She thought I wasn't **paying attention**, but I was! I'm from Oman. There, we don't maintain eye contact with people of different genders—I'm male and my teacher is female. Has anyone else had an experience like this?

👤 Lilia

5 My experience is **similar**, but a little different. I'm from Ukraine, and I just moved to Canada. A few weeks ago, I was talking with a colleague. Strangely, she backed away[3] from me while we were talking. I didn't know what the problem was. Well, I found out that people in Canada need more personal space—that's the space between you and another person. Standing close to them makes them **uncomfortable**. Where I'm from, people stand pretty close to each other when they're talking.

[1]**tone of voice** (phr) the strength and sound of your voice
[2]**colleague** (n) someone you work with
[3]**back away** (v phr) to move slowly backwards

B MAIN IDEAS Complete the summary of the article.

body   eye   eyes   space   voice   words

Communicating is more than just using

[1]_____. Tone of [2]_____ and

[3]_____ language are also important.

In Japan, for example, you look at someone's

[4]_____ to know if they have a

question. Body language means different

things for different cultures. For some

cultures [5]_____ contact and personal

[6]_____ are important.

READING SKILL Understand charts

Charts make it easier to understand the ideas in a text. When you see a chart, first read the title. This tells you the topic of the chart. Next look at labels or numbers to see what the chart is measuring. Then look for a key. It explains what the colors, lines, or symbols mean. Finally, scan the text to see where the information in the chart is mentioned, and think about how it supports the ideas in the text.

C APPLY Look at the pie chart in the article. Choose the correct answers.

1. The key includes information about what the **colors / lines / symbols** mean.

2. We mostly communicate through **words / tone of voice / body language**.

3. The chart supports the ideas in paragraph **1 / 2 / 3**.

D DETAILS Read the statements. Write T for *True*, F for *False*, or NG for *Not Given*.

1. _____ "Read the air" is a saying from Japan.

2. _____ In Japan, when someone wants to ask a question, they usually raise their hand.

3. _____ In Oman, people of the same gender usually maintain eye contact when they are speaking.

4. _____ In Ukraine, people usually stand far apart from each other when they are talking.

5. _____ Canadians often maintain eye contact when they are talking.

CRITICAL THINKING Personalize new information

After you read an article, connect any new information to your life. This can help you better understand the point that the writer is trying to make and help you remember information.

REFLECT   Analyze your body language.

Choose the word(s) to make each statement true for you. Then discuss your answers in a small group.

1. I am **comfortable / uncomfortable** maintaining eye contact with people.
2. People in my culture stand **close / not so close** when speaking to someone they don't know.
3. People in my culture use **tone of voice / body language** more when talking about feelings.
4. I'm **good / not good** at "reading the air."

An English teacher in Ankara, Turkey

PREPARE TO READ

A VOCABULARY Write a word from the box next to each definition. Use a dictionary if necessary.

affect (v)	certain (adj)	existing (adj)	influence (n)	represent (v)
as a result (conj)	evolve (v)	factor (n)	lead to (v phr)	silent (adj)

1. _____: to be a sign or symbol for something

2. _____: to cause a change in something or someone

3. _____: the power to change something or someone

4. _____: to cause to happen, to result in

5. _____: therefore

6. _____: not making any sound; not spoken

7. _____: sure to happen

8. _____: being real or present

9. _____: a cause of something

10. _____: to change over a long period of time

B PERSONALIZE Discuss these questions with a partner.

1. In the past, people traveled to other countries a lot less than they do today. Do you think travel is a **factor** in language change? Explain.

2. What words in English have **silent** letters (e.g., _knife_)?

3. How has technology **affected** your learning in the last few years?

REFLECT Identify ways that language changes.

You are going to read about how English has changed over time. What are some differences in the way you communicate and the way your grandparents communicated at your age? Write your ideas. Then discuss your ideas with a partner.

1. Phrases and expressions:

_____

2. Body language:

_____

3. Forms of communication:

_____

EVOLVING ENGLISH

A woman texts as she passes a mural of William Shakespeare near the Globe theatre in London. Shakespeare wrote many famous plays. He also created over 1,700 words that are still used in English today.

A PREDICT What do you think the article is mostly about?

a. A new technology that changed the English language

b. How English has changed a lot and will continue to change

c. Why it is a good thing for languages like English to change

1   Languages **evolve**. This is very true of English. An English writer from a thousand years ago would not know most of the words used in English today. Two of the main **factors** that **lead to** changes in the English language are new inventions and the **influence** of other languages.

2   New technology—particularly[1] the Internet—has changed the way we use English. The Internet has produced many new words such as *hashtag*, *selfie*, and *spam*. It's even given us new phrases, like "I tagged you in a post" or "She friended me." In addition, the Internet has changed the meanings of some **existing** words. For example, the word *tweet* means a sound a small bird makes. Now, it more often means a short message posted on Twitter.

3   Earlier inventions also **affected** the English language. The most important was the printing press. The printing press first came to England in the late 15th century. Suddenly, it became much easier to create and distribute[2] books. People quickly realized how inconsistent[3] the spelling was in these books. Before the printing press, there was no fixed way to spell many words. For example, the word *friend* could be spelled *friend, frend,* or *frind*. Book publishers decided to make some spelling rules for English. One change they made was to the letter *v*. *V* used to have both a *u* sound and a *v* sound. With the new spelling rules, the letter began to **represent** only the *v* sound.

The printing press was invented in Germany in 1440 by Johannes Gutenberg.

Number of English Speakers Worldwide
(Millions)

■ 379	753

■ Native speakers   ■ Non-native speakers

Source: babble.com

4   Non-English speakers played an important role in how English evolved. Until the 10th century, the language in England sounded and looked like German. We now call this language Old English. Within 300 years, though, English had completely changed. First, the Norse-speaking Vikings came. From them, we have many useful words like *leg*, *sky*, and *take*. Old English also adopted[4] Norse grammar. For example, the pronouns *they, their,* and *them* come from Norse. Later, French-speakers from northern France arrived in England. **As a result**, over 10,000 French words entered the English vocabulary. During this time, the pronunciation of many words changed, but the spelling didn't always change. This helps explain why English spelling can be so difficult today. For example, the word *beef* is spelled like it sounds in English even though it came from the French word *boeuf*. However, the word *people* is spelled with a **silent** letter o. This spelling came from the old French word *pople* and the *o* was not dropped.

5   How will English evolve in the next 100 years? It's hard to know for sure. It's possible it will become simpler. For instance, some experts think that count and non-count nouns will be the same. So, we will use plural forms like *informations* and *homeworks* in the future. Other experts think that technology will be the main factor. New technology may remove the need for some words altogether. Emojis may replace the need for actual words in much of our writing, for example. With over 1.1 billion speakers, we can be **certain** that English will never stop evolving.

[1]**particularly** (adv) especially

[2]**distribute** (v) to give out

[3]**inconsistent** (adj) not matching; different

[4]**adopt** (v) to use and make one's own

B MAIN IDEAS Write the paragraph number (2–5) next to the heading that describes it. Two headings are extra.

a. _____ The Influence of Other Languages   d. _____ Fixing the Spelling

b. _____ New Words from New Technology   e. _____ Will English Still Evolve?

c. _____ A Global Language   f. _____ Shakespeare's Language

C DETAILS Complete the chart with one word or number for each blank. Use words from the reading passage. Then check your answers with a partner.

Factors that caused English to evolve	Effects on the English language
The Internet	▶ Made new [1]_____ and [2]_____ ▶ Changed the [3]_____ of a few [4]_____ words
The [5]_____ press	▶ Helped create [6]_____ rules for many words
The influence of [7]_____ speakers	▶ Old English took some pronouns from [8]_____ ▶ More than [9]_____ words from French ▶ Spelling mostly stayed the same, but the [10]_____ of words changed

D Look at the bar chart in the reading and answer the questions.

1. What information does the larger bar show? _____

2. How many non-native English speakers are there? _____

3. Which paragraph of the article does the chart support? _____

REFLECT   Predict how English will evolve.

Answer the questions in your notebook. Then share your answers with a partner.

1. According to the article, the English language may become simpler in the future. Do you think this will happen? Explain.

2. What are some words that you think we might stop using? Explain.

3. What is one change in English grammar or spelling that you would like to see happen?

WRITE

A restaurant in
Sophia, Bulgaria

UNIT TASK Write a paragraph about a cultural misunderstanding.

You are going to write a story similar to one of the comments in "Can You 'Read the Air?'" Your story should tell about a misunderstanding between people from different cultures. Use the ideas, vocabulary, and skills from the unit.

A MODEL Read the paragraph. What was the funny misunderstanding? What lesson did the writer learn? Discuss your answers with a partner.

Where *Yes* Means *No*

I had a funny misunderstanding that taught me a good lesson. It happened when I was visiting a small town in Bulgaria. One day, I went to a local restaurant. The server came to take my order. I don't speak Bulgarian, so I pointed at a sandwich on the menu. The server shook her head from side to side. I was confused because other people at the restaurant were eating sandwiches. I pointed at the soup. Again, the server shook her head. Clearly, though, people were having soup. While I was looking at the menu for a third time, she looked at me strangely. Then I remembered. In Bulgaria, people shake their heads from side to side for "yes," and they nod their heads up and down for "no." I laughed at myself and said I was sorry. Then I ordered a sandwich *and* soup. Now I know. It's always important to understand the body language of the country that you are visiting.

B ANALYZE THE MODEL Complete the outline of the model paragraph.

Title: Where *Yes* Means *No*

Topic sentence: I had a funny misunderstanding that taught me a good lesson.

First event: The server came to take my order.

    Details: I _____ at a sandwich.

    The server _____ her head from side to side. I was confused.

Second event: So, I _____

    Details: The server _____

    _____

Third event: The server looked at me _____.

    Detail: In Bulgaria, people _____ to mean "yes"

    and nod their heads up and down to mean "no."

Fourth event: I laughed at myself and ordered _____.

Concluding sentence: It's always important to understand the

_____.

WRITING SKILL Write a topic sentence

Most paragraphs have one main idea. The **topic sentence** states the main idea.
It tells the reader what the paragraph is about. A topic sentence has two parts. It
states your topic, and it states your approach to the topic. The approach is called
the controlling idea.

> _Eye contact_ can _mean different things in different cultures._
>   topic   controlling idea

The **controlling idea** tells the reader what information will be in the paragraph.
It should not be too general or too specific. If it is too general, the reader won't
know what the paragraph is about. If it is too specific, the reader doesn't need to
read the paragraph.

Too general: *Eye contact can mean different things.*
Too specific: *The meaning of eye contact can vary in different cultures, indicating*
                  anger in one place and friendliness in another.

C APPLY Look at the topic sentence from the model paragraph. Write its topic
and controlling idea.

Topic: _____

Controlling idea: _____

D APPLY Underline the topic and double-underline the controlling idea in these topic sentences.

1. Body language is an important part of communication for several reasons.
2. Facial expressions can mean different things in different countries.
3. Using an English-English dictionary can help students of English in many ways.

E APPLY Read the topic sentences. Write C for *Correct*, TG for *Too General*, and TS for *Too Specific*.

1. _____ I had a communication problem with a friend when we were discussing the best way to do homework.
2. _____ I had a communication problem with a friend once.
3. _____ I had a communication problem with a friend because I told her that the best time to do homework is right after class.

F NOTICE THE GRAMMAR Look back at the model paragraph. Underline the verbs that talk about the past. What two forms do you notice? How do they differ in meaning? Tell a partner.

GRAMMAR Simple past and past continuous

We use the **simple past** to talk about events that started and ended in the past.

*Two years ago, I **visited** Peru. I **didn't go** to Machu Picchu.*

We use the **past continuous** to talk about events that were in progress in the past.

*When I went to Machu Pichu, I **wasn't traveling** alone. I **was traveling** with a friend.*

In narratives, we often use the past continuous with *when* or *while* to indicate an event (past continuous) that was interrupted by another event (simple past).

***While** we **were driving** to Machu Picchu, the bus **broke down**.*

*I **was sleeping when** it **happened**.*

G GRAMMAR Choose the correct verbs to complete the sentences.

1. A thousand years ago, English **sounded / was sounding** like German.
2. I didn't feel comfortable. My classmate **stood / was standing** too close to me.
3. My friend and I **met / were meeting** for lunch yesterday.
4. While I **drove / was driving** to work, I **got / was getting** a flat tire.
5. I **got / was getting** to work early yesterday.
6. I **learned / was learning** a lot about body language while

   I **traveled / was traveling** around the world.

H GRAMMAR Complete the sentences with the verbs in parentheses. Use the simple past or past continuous. Sometimes both may be correct.

1. The woman in the video _____ (make) funny faces while she _____ (dance).

2. The woman in the video _____ (have) a problem with her friend. When she _____ (make) the sound "hmm," her friend _____ (think) it had a different meaning.

3. In the article in reading 1, a woman _____ (write) a comment about personal space. She said that she _____ (stand) too close to a colleague while they _____ (speak). She _____ (be) happy when she finally _____ (understand) the problem.

I EDIT Read the paragraph. Find and correct six errors with the simple past and past continuous.

A Hug or a Kiss on the Cheek?

I have an awkward misunderstanding a few years ago that ended happily. I am taking English classes in New York City. One of my classmates, Valentina, was from Switzerland. Our teacher asked us to work together a lot. After a couple of weeks, we became friends. One day, we decided to get together for coffee after school. When I waiting in line to order, Valentina walked up to me. I knew that in the United States, friends hug each other. I open up my arms to hug her. After the hug, I started to back away, but she moves closer. Then, we hit our heads together. She explained that she tried to kiss me on the cheek. People in Switzerland kiss each other on the cheeks three times. We are still friends and we often laugh about that day.

Women greeting one another

PLAN & WRITE

J **BRAINSTORM** Think of a misunderstanding with someone from a different culture. It may be the one from the video or one you know about. What happened? Write your answers to the questions.

1. Who had the misunderstanding? _____

2. Where did it happen? _____

3. What were you (or someone else) doing when it happened? _____

   _____

4. What was the misunderstanding about? Was it related to body language, vocabulary, tone of voice, or something else?

   _____

   _____

5. What were the main events of the story? _____

   _____

   _____

   _____

6. How did the story end?

   _____

   _____

7. What was the lesson of this story?

   _____

   _____

WRITING TIP

A narrative paragraph tells a story in the order the events happened. The topic sentence tells the main idea, or what the story is about. The middle sentences describe the background (where you were, what you were doing, who you were with) and tell the main events of the story. The concluding sentence explains how the story ends, and it often has a lesson that you learned.

K OUTLINE Complete the outline. Use your notes from activity J.

Title:_____

Topic sentence: _____

First event: _____

    Details: _____

    _____

Second event: _____

    Details: _____

    _____

Third event: _____

    Details: _____

    _____

Concluding sentence: _____

L FIRST DRAFT Use your outline to write a first draft of your paragraph.

M REVISE Use this list as you write your second draft.

☐ Does your topic sentence introduce the main idea of your paragraph? Does it include a controlling idea?

☐ Do your detail sentences give more information about each event?

☐ Did you explain the reason for the misunderstanding?

☐ Does your paragraph have a concluding sentence?

N EDIT Use this list as you write your final draft.

☐ Did you use the simple past and past continuous correctly?

☐ Do your subjects and verbs agree?

☐ Did you spell all the words correctly?

☐ Did you use correct punctuation?

O FINAL DRAFT Reread your paragraph and correct any errors. Then submit it to your teacher.

REFLECT

A Check (✓) the Reflect activities you can do and the academic skills you can use.

- ☐ brainstorm ways we communicate
- ☐ analyze your body language
- ☐ identify ways that language changes
- ☐ predict how English will evolve
- ☐ write a paragraph about a cultural misunderstanding

- ☐ understand charts
- ☐ write a topic sentence
- ☐ simple past and past continuous
- ☐ personalize new information

B Write the vocabulary words from the unit in the correct column. Add any other words that you learned. Circle words you still need to practice.

NOUN	VERB	ADJECTIVE	ADVERB & OTHER

C Reflect on the ideas in the unit as you answer these questions.

1. What is the most interesting idea about language that you learned in this unit?

_____

_____

_____

2. What ideas or skills in this unit will be most useful to you in the future? Explain.

_____

_____

_____

3 | IS FEAR FUN?

An audience watching
a 3-D horror movie

CONNECT TO THE TOPIC

1. Do you enjoy movies like the one people in the photo are watching?

2. Do you think fear can be fun?

WATCH

Alex Honnold, the strongest free solo climber in the world

FREE SOLO TRAILER

A PREVIEW Answer the questions with a partner.

1. Who is the man in the photo? Why is he special?

2. A movie trailer is a preview or advertisement for a movie. What do you think the movie *Free Solo* is about?

B Read the statements. Then watch the trailer for *Free Solo*. Write T for *True* or F for *False*. ▶3.1

Free Solo...

1. _____ is about a climbing competition.

2. _____ has interviews with some of Honnold's family.

3. _____ teaches various climbing styles.

4. _____ is a documentary.

C Do you want to watch *Free Solo*? Write your reasons. Then discuss with a partner.

_____

_____

PREPARE TO READ

A VOCABULARY Read the sentences. Then write the bold words next to their definitions.

My greatest **challenge** at school this year was learning how to edit video.

Alex Honnold's story is **inspiring**. He shows what is possible with hard work.

I can't breathe when I'm in a high place. I find it very **scary**.

The view from the top of the mountain was **incredible**.

The student won a prize for her film. It was a great **achievement**.

On the climber's first **attempt** up the mountain, he used ropes to be safe.

You take a great **risk** when you free solo.

The filmmakers didn't want to **put pressure on** Honnold to do the climb.

The cameras, falling rock, or a bird are all things that could **distract** a climber.

You must **concentrate** when you are editing video content.

1. _____ (adj) amazing

2. _____ (adj) causing a feeling of wanting to do something

3. _____ (v phr) to make someone feel that they have to do something

4. _____ (n) a successful completion of a task

5. _____ (v) to take someone's attention away

6. _____ (n) an effort or a try

7. _____ (n) a chance of losing something important

8. _____ (v) to think carefully about something

9. _____ (n) a task that is difficult to do

10. _____ (adj) causing strong feelings of fear

B PERSONALIZE Discuss your answers to these questions with a partner.

1. Describe your greatest **achievement**. What was it? When was it?

2. What **challenges** did you have reaching this achievement?

REFLECT Assess why we do things that cause fear.

Before you read a review of *Free Solo*, consider why people do things that cause fear. Check (✓) the reasons. Add your own ideas. Then share your ideas with a partner.

☐ They like the feeling.

☐ They have a sense of achievement.

☐ Other people put pressure on them.

☐ _____

☐ They are inspired by others.

☐ They don't think it's scary.

☐ They like a challenge.

☐ _____

FREE SOLO

Climber aims high in nail-biting documentary

Alex Honnold free soloing El Capitan in Yosemite National Park, California, USA

A PREVIEW Read the title and skim the first paragraph. How does the writer feel about the movie? Underline the words or phrases that give the reviewer's opinion.

3.1

1   Imagine you are climbing a mountain that is a thousand feet high. You have no ropes. You just have your body and your wits[1]. This is called free soloing. *Free Solo* is a movie about Alex Honnold's **attempt** to free solo El Capitan. El Capitan is a 3,200 foot (975 m) high rock in Yosemite National Park, California. *Free Solo* is a great movie about an amazing **achievement**.

2   No one has ever free soloed El Capitan before—with good reason. It is very dangerous. Less than one percent of rock climbers free solo. Free soloing up El Capitan is even more dangerous. Some of its ledges[2] are only as wide as two coins. In some places, there are no ledges at all to put your feet on. Because of the **risks**, Honnold carefully plans the route. We see him practicing every step. His ability to **concentrate** and complete such a difficult climb is **inspiring**. However, knowing that Honnold is one misstep from death makes *Free Solo* difficult to watch. Some moments were so **scary** that I wanted to look away—but I didn't because the movie is so good.

3   The scenes[3] of Honnold's climb are amazing because of the great film makers. Co-director Jimmy Chin describes the **challenge** of finding cinematographers who could also climb. During filming, they all climbed El Capitan. Each person had to carry around fifty pounds of cameras. Chin, who is also Honnold's friend, explains how they were scared to make a sound. One sneeze could **distract** Honnold. This could cause him to fall. "It's hard not to imagine your friend falling… to his death," Chin says in the movie. Chin worried that the cameras **put pressure on** Honnold. He thought about stopping the movie. In the end, however, he realized that Honnold was going to climb—with or without the cameras.

4   The movie asks an important question: Why does Honnold free solo? The movie answers this with some interesting interviews. Honnold's mother explains, "When he's free soloing…he feels most alive." Co-director Elizabeth Chai Vasarhelyi says, "As a kid, it was scarier for him to speak to another person and ask them to be a partner than to go out by himself." Whatever the reason, Honnold clearly loves to free solo. He shows no real fear. In the movie, he gets an MRI scan[4] of his brain. The results suggest that he doesn't feel fear as much as other people. Perhaps Honnold is fearless.

5   *Free Solo* is an amazing movie. It shows an **incredible** achievement. It also shows the person who did it and the people who helped. It's not surprising that it won so many awards. I recommend that you see it.

---

[1]**wits** (n) ability to think quickly

[2]**ledge** (n) a narrow surface on the side of a mountain or a building

[3]**scene** (n) part of a movie in which events happen in the same place

[4]**MRI scan** (n phr) an image of the inside of the body made by a large machine

B MAIN IDEAS Choose the three main reasons the reviewer liked the movie *Free Solo*.

a. The scenes are well filmed.

b. Watching the cinematographers free soloing is surprising.

c. The movie is scary but in a good way.

d. It teaches people how to free solo.

e. The interviews tell a lot about the people in the movie.

C DETAILS Match the first part of each sentence (1–4) with the correct ending (a–e). There is one extra answer.

1. Chin stayed quiet because ____

2. Chin continued filming because ____

3. Honnold free solos because ____

4. Honnold isn't scared because ____

a. Honnold asked him to.

b. he didn't want to distract Honnold.

c. it makes him feel alive.

d. he doesn't feel fear like other people.

e. Honnold would free solo anyway.

READING SKILL Make inferences

Writers often suggest an idea without stating it directly. When you make inferences or infer, you make a conclusion based on other information in the text. For example, the reviewer states that "*Free solo* means to climb without any help, ropes, or equipment." We can infer, then, that normal climbing includes help, ropes, and equipment.

D APPLY Write *I* if you can infer the information from the reading. Write *NI* if you can't infer it.

1. _____ There are many cinematographers who can also climb. (Paragraph 3)

2. _____ Honnold pressured Chin to make the film. (Paragraph 3)

3. _____ When he was a boy, Alex was probably shy. (Paragraph 4)

4. _____ An MRI scan can show a person's reactions to fear. (Paragraph 4)

REFLECT   Understand fear in your life.

Write answers to the questions in your notebook. Then discuss with a partner.

1. How might fear protect you from danger?

2. Do you enjoy sports with risk, like climbing, down hill skiing, or other?

3. Do you want to try free soloing?

PREPARE TO READ

A VOCABULARY Read the definitions. Complete the sentences with the correct form of the words.

character (n) a person in a story or movie

excitement (n) a strong, pleasant feeling

experience (v) to have something happen to you

intense (adj) very strong in feeling

preference (n) wanting one thing more than another

relieved (adj) happy because something bad didn't happen

response (n) something you say, feel, or do because of something else

suffer (v) to experience pain or discomfort

survive (v) to continue to live

symptom (n) a sign in your body of an illness or other problem

1. Actors often change the way they look to fit the _____ they're playing.

2. Most people are _____ when a scary situation is over.

3. Many children _____ from nightmares.

4. Rock climbers sometimes fall, but they usually _____ because they use ropes.

5. During _____ parts of movies, viewers often hold their breath.

6. In a horror movie, most characters _____ some terrible event.

7. Some people love the feeling of _____ from being on a rollercoaster.

8. Some _____ of a cold are sneezing, coughing, and a sore throat.

9. I don't like horror movies, so my _____ is to watch a comedy tonight.

10. People have different _____ to scary events in movies. Some might scream, and others might look away.

REFLECT   Rate situations that cause fear.

Before you read more about fear, think about the situations you find scary. Rate how scary each situation is to you. Write a number between 1 and 5 (1= not scary and 5 = very scary). Add your own ideas. Then discuss with a partner.

_____ watching a scary movie   _____ being high up   _____ clowns

_____ seeing a spider   _____ being in total darkness   _____ _____

_____ going on a roller coaster   _____ flying   _____ _____

FEAR IS FUN...
FOR SOME

A PREDICT Read the title and the headings of the article. What do you think the article is mainly about? Choose the best answer.

a. Why most people should avoid activities that cause fear

b. Why some people enjoy activities that cause fear

c. Why being afraid is bad for you

🎧 3.2

1   Picture this: You are on a rollercoaster ride. Your heart is beating fast. You scream. We all know the **symptoms** of fear, but why do we feel it? And why do some people enjoy it?

WHAT HAPPENS WHEN WE FEEL FEAR

2   When we are scared, we **experience** a fight-or-flight **response**. Our bodies get ready either to defend ourselves (fight) or to run away (flight). The release of hormones[1] in our brains causes this response. One hormone, adrenaline, causes our hearts to beat faster. More blood goes to our muscles to make us stronger. In addition, we become alert[2] to everything around us. We also breathe faster. All of these changes happen in order to help us **survive** danger.

WHY FEAR CAN FEEL GOOD

3   While fear is a negative emotion, it can also feel good. Watching a scary movie produces a fight-or-flight response. However, we usually watch movies in a safe space, such as a living room. We also often watch with other people, such as our friends. Our brain quickly understands that the scary events are not real. There's no danger. Instead, we feel the **excitement** of the adrenaline in our bodies without the need to really fight or run away.

4   Our fight-or-flight response quickly changes. Sociologist Dr. Margee Kerr notes that after a short time, the effect of the adrenaline goes away. Then, according to Kerr, our fight-or-flight response "floods our brains with feel-good chemicals." One of these

A couple on a
roller coaster

is dopamine. Dopamine plays a role in how we feel pleasure. Once a scary scene ends, we have an **intense** feeling of pleasure. We are **relieved** that the **character** survived and got away from the scary monster. Kerr also says that many people enjoy being scared because "it leaves them with a sense of confidence after it's over." For example, when a rollercoaster ride ends, we feel proud that we made it all the way to the end.

WHEN FEAR ISN'T FUN

5   Some of us enjoy being scared, but many of us don't. Around ten percent of the population loves feeling scared. However, most people don't enjoy it at all. One possible reason for this is that people respond to dopamine differently. People with weaker responses don't feel as positive when they are scared. Another reason is that most of us don't like seeing other people **suffer**. This is true even when we know the others aren't really suffering. They're just actors. These responses can make scary movies unpleasant.

6   Whether you find scary movies fun or not, there is a biological explanation for your **preference**. For those who enjoy being scared, watching scary movies is a safe way to feel fear. For those who don't like watching these movies, now you have a science-based reason not to.

¹**hormones** (n) chemicals in your body that affect body functions, including growth and mood

²**alert** (adj) completely aware

B MAIN IDEAS Write the correct paragraph number (2-5) next to its main idea.

a. _____ There are scientific reasons why some people don't enjoy being scared.

b. _____ Our bodies react to fear in specific ways.

c. _____ Watching scary movies has several positive effects on the brain.

d. _____ Fear can feel positive when we know we aren't in danger.

C DETAILS What happens to our bodies when we feel fear? Complete each sentence with up to two words from the article.

1. When we are scared, adrenaline makes our hearts _____.

2. Our muscles get stronger because more _____ goes to them.

3. We _____ more quickly.

4. When the danger is gone, our brain releases _____, such as dopamine.

5. Dopamine gives us a feeling of _____.

6. People _____ to dopamine in different ways.

D Read the sentences. Choose the best inference.

When we are scared, we experience a fight-or-flight response. Our bodies get ready either to defend ourselves (fight) or to run away (flight).

a. The fight-or-flight response helps us survive dangerous situations.

b. We also experience the fight-or-flight response with other emotions.

c. The fight-or-flight response is not very helpful in dangerous situations.

CRITICAL THINKING Synthesize information

When you synthesize, you combine and analyze information from two or more sources. Synthesizing helps you understand how different pieces of information are connected.

REFLECT   Synthesize information from the readings.

Why do you think Alex Honnold enjoys free soloing? Choose the reason you feel is right. Then discuss it with a partner. Support your opinion with information from the readings.

a. He likes feeling fear.

b. He doesn't have a typical fight-or-flight response.

c. He can focus on the exciting challenge, not the fear.

WRITE

Movie poster for
A Quiet Place

UNIT TASK   Write a movie review.

You are going to write a short review of a movie you liked. Use the ideas, vocabulary, and skills from this unit.

A MODEL   Read the review. Underline the word(s) in the title and topic sentence that tell you the writer's opinion.

A Quiet Place: Scarily Good

A Quiet Place is an amazing movie with great actors and scary scenes. The movie features monsters that attack people when they hear a noise. But the movie is really about a normal family who is trying to survive. Eventually, the family learns a strategy that helps them beat the aliens. The first thing I like about the movie is the quality of the acting. For example, the father, played by John Krasinski, is very caring. We see and feel that he really wants to save his family. Krasinski, who also wrote and directed the movie, won awards for his work in the film. Another good thing about the movie is that it's very scary. There are many moments with the monsters that have you on the edge of your seat*. The scariest moment, though, is when the mother must be silent while having a baby. If you like scary movies with good acting, see *A Quiet Place*. I recommend it.

***on the edge of your seat** (phr) very excited

WRITING SKILL Write supporting ideas and details

As you learned in Unit 1, a paragraph includes supporting ideas and details. **Supporting ideas** develop the topic sentence. **Details** include facts, examples, or explanations that give more information about each supporting idea. Look at these notes for a paragraph that reviews *The Avengers: Endgame*.

> **Topic sentence:** *The Avengers: Endgame* is a well-made superhero movie with a good plot.
>
> **Supporting Idea 1:** Excellent special effects
> Detail (fact): Movie cost over $300m to make
> Detail (example): CGI "Smart Hulk" looks very realistic
>
> **Supporting Idea 2:** Emotional story
> Detail (explanation): Superheroes risk danger in order to save others
> Detail (example): Iron Man suffers in order to save the universe

B ANALYZE THE MODEL Complete the outline of the model paragraph.

Title: _____

Topic sentence: *A Quiet Place* is an amazing movie with _____
_____ .

Description of movie: The movie is about _____ .
_____ .

Supporting idea 1: The first thing to recommend about the movie is
_____ .

    Detail: _____

    Detail: _____

    Detail: _____

Supporting idea 2: Another thing that is good about the movie is
_____ .

    Detail: _____

    Detail: _____

Concluding sentence: If you like scary movies _____
_____

> **WRITING TIP**
>
> Writers often give background information after the topic sentence. This helps the reader more clearly understand the topic. In a paragraph about a movie, for example, you can give a brief description of the movie and the type of film it is.

C Which of the details in the model paragraph are examples?
Which are facts? Which are explanations? Discuss with a partner.

D APPLY Read the topic sentence. Then write SI next to the three *Supporting Ideas* and D next to the three *Details*.

Topic sentence: *Free Solo* is fascinating, beautiful, and expertly made.

1. _____ The scenery in *Free Solo* is wonderful.

2. _____ He's very calm, and he never seems nervous or scared.

3. _____ The subject of the documentary, Alex Honnold, is an unusual person.

4. _____ The movie-making techniques are really amazing.

5. _____ The camera people were climbing with equipment right next to Honnold during the filming.

6. _____ As you watch Honnold climb, you see beautiful views of Yosemite National Park.

GRAMMAR Adjective clauses

Clauses are groups of words that have a subject and a verb. Adjective clauses give more information about nouns. They add detail and allow you to combine ideas into one sentence. Adjective clauses begin with a relative pronoun (*who* or *that* for people and *that* or *which* for things).

In a **subject adjective clause**, the relative pronoun is the subject of the clause. The verb in the clause agrees with the noun that comes before the relative pronoun:

> The actor **who does the best job** is Robert Downey Jr.
>   relative pronoun + verb

In an **object adjective clause**, the relative pronoun is the object. A subject and a verb follow the pronoun. The relative pronoun can be omitted in object adjective clauses.

> The movie **(that) I saw last week** was Frozen II.
> (relative pronoun) + subject + verb

E GRAMMAR Underline the adjective clauses and circle the relative pronouns. Then write S if it's a *Subject Clause* or O if it's an *Object Clause*.

1. _____ The movie features monsters that attack people when they hear a noise.

2. _____ It's really about a normal family who is trying to survive.

3. _____ They are a normal family that viewers can connect with.

4. _____ They learn a strategy that helps them beat the monsters.

5. _____ Scary scenes and characters that we can relate to make it a great movie.

F GRAMMAR Complete the sentences. Write all possible relative pronouns (*that, who, which,* or Ø, if no pronoun is needed).

1. The Brazilian actress _____ I like the best is Alice Braga Moraes.

2. The filmmakers _____ made *Free Solo* are married.

3. Watching movies _____ cause you fear can actually produce good feelings.

4. The Korean movie _____ won the Academy Award was called *Parasite*.

5. The director _____ Helena Bonham Carter likes to work with the most is Tim Burton.

G GRAMMAR Complete each sentence with an adjective clause. Use some subject clauses and some object clauses.

1. I watch movies _____.

2. An actor _____.

3. I don't watch movies _____.

4. A risk _____ I _____.

5. The movie is about a hero _____.

H EDIT Read the movie review. Find and correct five errors with adjective clauses.

Avengers: End Game—Movie of the Year

The movie who I really liked this year was *Avengers: Endgame*. It is a well-made superhero movie, with interesting characters and great acting. The movie is about how the Avengers—including Robert Downey Jr. as Iron Man—go back in time to find some special stones. The stones will bring people back to life. The first thing I noticed about the movie is the excellent special effects. For example, the "Smart Hulk" character looks extremely realistic. In fact, he looks just like Mark Ruffalo, the actor plays The Hulk. *Avengers: Endgame* also has great characters who are real heroes. Several characters make difficult choices in order to help others. Hawkeye and Black Widow, for example, have to lose something who they love it. Finally, the acting in *Avengers: Endgame* is great. The actor he does the best job is Robert Downey Jr.. He is both funny and very sad at the same time. In fact, audiences around the world cried during Iron Man's final scene. *Avengers: Endgame* is really worth seeing—I recommend it!

PLAN & WRITE

I BRAINSTORM Complete the chart with information about two movies you like. Write the parts of the movie you like and what was good about those parts.

	Movie:	Movie:
Plot/story		
Actors		
Characters		
Setting/scenes		
Script/dialogue		
Special effects/music/direction		
Other		

A drive-in movie theater at Tottori Port in western Japan

J OUTLINE Choose a movie from activity I, and complete the outline.

Title: _____

Topic sentence: _____

Description of movie: _____

Supporting idea 1: _____

    Details: _____

    _____

Supporting idea 2: _____

    Details: _____

    _____

Supporting idea 3: _____

    Details: _____

    _____

Concluding sentence: _____

_____

K FIRST DRAFT Use your outline to write a first draft of your paragraph.

L REVISE Use this list as you write your second draft.

☐ Does your topic sentence include the topic and controlling idea?

☐ Did you include a short description of the movie?

☐ Does your paragraph have two or more supporting ideas?

☐ Does each supporting idea have one or two details?

☐ Are all your sentences about the topic?

M EDIT Use this list as you write your final draft.

☐ Did you use adjective clauses correctly?

☐ Do your subjects and verbs agree?

☐ Did you spell all the words correctly?

☐ Did you use correct punctuation?

N FINAL DRAFT Reread your movie review and correct any errors. Then submit it to your teacher.

REFLECT

A Check (✓) the Reflect activities you can do and the academic skills you can use.

- ☐ assess why people do things that cause fear
- ☐ understand fear in your life
- ☐ rank situations that cause fear
- ☐ synthesize information from the readings
- ☐ write a movie review
- ☐ make inferences
- ☐ write supporting ideas and details
- ☐ adjective clauses
- ☐ synthesize information

B Write the vocabulary words from the unit in the correct column. Add any other words that you learned. Circle the words you still need to practice.

NOUN	VERB	ADJECTIVE	ADVERB & OTHER

C Reflect on the ideas in the unit as you answer these questions.

1. What is the most surprising thing you learned about fear and entertainment in this unit?

_____

_____

_____

2. What ideas or skills in this unit will be most useful to you in the future? Explain.

_____

_____

_____

UNIT

4 | THE ART
IN SCIENCE

Dutch artist Berndnaut Smilde creates clouds in various places, such as this one in the Green Room of the Veterans Building in San Francisco, California, USA.

IN THIS UNIT

- ▸ Match skills to STEM jobs
- ▸ Evaluate STEAM careers
- ▸ Compare humans with technology
- ▸ Assess robot art
- ▸ Write a paragraph about a graph

SKILLS

READING
Identify purpose and audience

WRITING
Summarize charts and graphs

GRAMMAR
Simple past and present perfect

CRITICAL THINKING
Assess features to form an opinion

CONNECT TO THE TOPIC

1. What do you think the unit title means?

2. How does the photo relate to the title of the unit?

THE MASTER OF FOLDS

A **PREDICT** Watch the first part of the video. Why is Robert Lang interested in origami? ▶ 4.1

    a. The challenge of making simple patterns interests him.

    b. He likes writing books and articles about origami.

    c. Doing origami shows him how other things can fold and unfold.

B Watch the complete video. Then match the first part of each sentence with the correct ending. ▶ 4.2

    1. Robert Lang created a round origami design _____

    2. He developed a small folded design _____

    3. He has used math to create _____

    4. Traditional origami usually requires _____

    5. Today's designs can require _____

    a. new designs.

    b. that fits into a rocket.

    c. up to 20 or 30 steps.

    d. up to a thousand steps.

    e. for a car's airbag.

C **PERSONALIZE** How could doing something artistic benefit your life? Discuss your answer with a partner.

Dr. Robert Lang folded this origami dragon from one single sheet of uncut paper.

PREPARE TO READ

A VOCABULARY Write the words next to their definitions. Use a dictionary if necessary.

annual (adj)	develop (v)	familiar (adj)	professional (adj)	specific (adj)
combine (v)	expression (n)	possibility (n)	quality (n)	trade (n)

1. _____: known to you

2. _____: how good something is

3. _____: relating to a a job that requires training or education

4. _____: to mix

5. _____: a show of how you think or feel

6. _____: opportunity

7. _____: a type of work that you are trained to do such as plumbing, construction, etc.

8. _____: yearly

9. _____: to design or create

10. _____: clearly defined

B PERSONALIZE Discuss these questions with a partner.

1. What career **possibilities** are you interested in?
2. What are some **specific** skills that you need for this career?
3. How can you **develop** these skills?

> REFLECT   Match skills to STEM jobs.
>
> Before you read about a few interesting careers, answer the questions. Then discuss with a partner.
>
> 1. What do you think is the main STEM skill (science, technology, engineering, or math) a person needs to be successful in each job?
>
>   architect _____   photographer _____
>
>   software developer _____   doctor/nurse _____
>
>   accountant _____   video game designer _____
>
> 2. Which jobs above require some knowledge of art?
>
>   _____

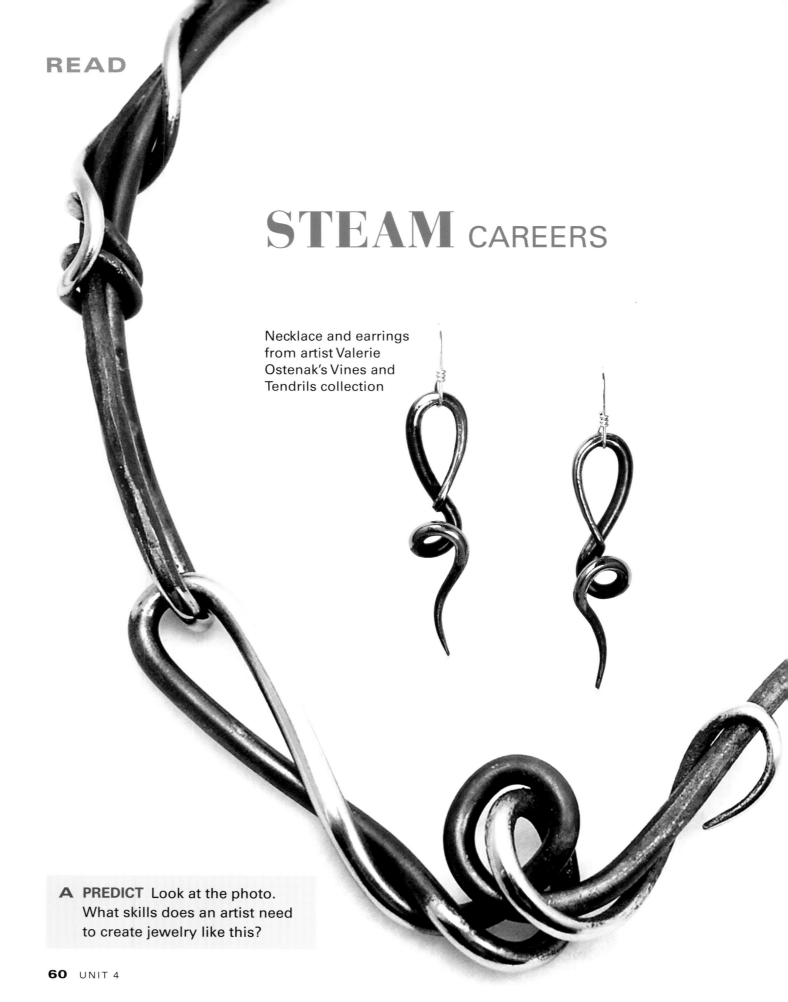

STEAM CAREERS

Necklace and earrings
from artist Valerie
Ostenak's Vines and
Tendrils collection

A PREDICT Look at the photo.
What skills does an artist need
to create jewelry like this?

1   What connects architects, mapmakers, and video game developers? They all have jobs that **combine** STEM skills and art. Careers that combine a STEM skill with art are called STEAM (Science, Technology, Engineering, Art, and Math) careers. You probably know something about STEAM jobs like these already. However, there are many more that you may not be **familiar** with. Check out three careers below.

SCIENTIFIC ANIMATOR

2   Do you like to draw? If so, you might like a career in scientific animation[1]. A scientific animator creates drawings or video clips of scientific processes. For example, they might animate how a part of the body works. Cameron Slayden is a scientific animator. He draws for *Science* magazine. He also **develops** short animations for TV shows about science. Slayden has a background in art and science. Like many scientific animators, he studied art and science in college. The average starting salary for this job is over $70,000 a year.

METALSMITH

3   Working with metal also combines art with science. Metalsmiths need artistic skills and a knowledge of science and math. Valerie Ostenak is a metalsmith. She works with steel, gold, and other metals. She makes jewelry, furniture, and sculptures. Ostenak studied science and thinks that "art is an **expression** of things that happen in nature." Metalsmiths can also work in repairing historic artifacts[2] for places like museums. You can learn to become a metalsmith at a college with an art program. You can also learn the skill at a **trade** school or by working with a **professional** metalsmith. Or, like Valerie Ostenak, you can study science. Metalsmiths earn about $40,000 a year when they start.

ACOUSTIC DESIGNER

4   If music is your passion, you might consider a career as an acoustic[3] designer. Acoustic designers often work in theaters and other places where music is recorded or played. They make sure that the sound **quality** in different spaces is good. Trevor Cox is an acoustic designer. To create the best sound, he considers a lot of different factors. For example, he thinks about the size of the room and the **specific** materials used for the walls. Some colleges offer degrees in acoustics. Often, these degrees involve classes in physics. The **annual** starting salary for an acoustic designer is about $100,000.

5   If you like the arts but don't want to be an artist, consider a STEAM career. There are so many **possibilities**, and the possibilities will continue to grow.

---

[1] **animation** (n) the process of making films that have pictures or objects that seem to move

[2] **artifacts** (n) objects that were made in the past and are important to history

[3] **acoustic** (adj) relating to sound

B MAIN IDEAS Choose the three main ideas of the article.

a. There are STEM jobs for people who are artistic.

b. Degrees in STEAM fields are offered at most colleges and universities.

c. There are different ways to learn the skills needed for STEAM jobs.

d. Acoustic designers have the highest starting salary.

e. In the future, there will be more STEAM jobs.

READING SKILL Identify purpose and audience

Texts are written for a particular purpose and for a particular audience. When you read a text, think about what the writer is trying to say (the **purpose**). The purpose can be to inform, to explain, to persuade, or to entertain. Then think about who they wrote it for (the **audience**). This will help you predict what the writer is going to say and how the text will be organized. It will also help you understand what details are important. For example, if the purpose of an article is to inform college students (audience) on how to interview well, the text will probably include tips on how to have a successful job interview.

C APPLY Choose the best answers. Then discuss with a partner.

1. Which audience do you think the article is mainly for?

   a. High-school students   b. College teachers   c. Workers in STEAM careers

2. What was the writer's purpose in writing the post?

   a. To give an opinion about the best STEAM careers

   b. To tell readers about different types of STEAM jobs

   c. To explain the pros and cons of different STEAM jobs

D DETAILS Complete the notes in the chart. Write one word or number from the article for each answer.

Career	Job description	Typical qualifications	Starting salary
Scientific animator	Draws and makes videos of scientific 1_____	College degree in art and 2_____	3_____
4_____	Makes jewelry, fixes historic 5_____	Get skills at a 6_____ school	7_____
Acoustic designer	Improves the acoustics in places where music is played	Usually study 8_____	9_____

REFLECT   Evaluate STEAM careers.

Write answers to the questions. Then discuss your answers in a group.

1. Which STEAM career was most interesting to you? _____

2. Why did you choose that career? _____

PREPARE TO READ

A VOCABULARY Complete the sentences with the correct form of the words. Use a dictionary if necessary.

ability (n)	attach (v)	field (n)	industrial (adj)	produce (v)
advance (v)	contest (n)	imagine (v)	original (adj)	realistic (adj)

1. Many robots are used for _____ purposes, such as building cars and making clothes.

2. You can _____ a file or photo when you send an email.

3. If a painting of a person is _____, it looks very much like that person.

4. Many college graduates enter the _____ of technology or engineering.

5. Close your eyes and _____ you are in your favorite place. What do you see?

6. Smartphone technology _____ every year. New smartphones have more features.

7. This edited photo looks nothing like the _____ photo.

8. Smartphone companies _____ over one billion smartphones each year.

9. Computers have the _____ to solve math problems much faster than people can.

10. The RoboCup is a _____ where teams of robots play soccer against each other.

B PERSONALIZE Discuss these questions with a partner.

1. What is a **contest** that you might enter (e.g., sports, academic, art, writing, music)?
2. Close your eyes and **imagine** the perfect day. What are you doing? Who are you with?
3. What is one of your strongest **abilities**?

REFLECT Compare humans with technology.

You are going to read about robot artists. Compare what people and technology can do. Write your ideas in the chart. Then discuss with a partner.

Fields	Abilities of people	Abilities of technology
car manufacturing		
health care		
cashier		
banking		

READ

ROBOT ARTISTS

A portrait created by the robot Cloudpainter, winner of the 2018 RobotArt competition

A PREVIEW Answer the questions.

1. Quickly scan the article for names of robot artists. How many different ones are mentioned? _____
   Underline the first time each robot is introduced.

2. Read the first paragraph. Who do you think the audience is for the article?
   a. engineers   b. general readers   c. art teachers

3. Why do you think the writer wrote the article for this audience?
   a. to give an opinion   b. to summarize research   c. to give information

1   Many artists use technology in their work. Some use 3D printers to make sculptures[1]. Others use drones[2] to take photographs. Recently, however, technology is creating its own artwork. Several robot artists are **advancing** the **fields** of both art and engineering.

2   ADA, a robot artist, can draw **realistic** portraits. ADA was named after Ada Lovelace, the first computer programmer. ADA was once an **industrial** robot. It used to make parts in a car factory. However, a company called Visionaire expanded its uses. Engineers **attached** a camera to ADA's arm. Computer programmers gave it the **ability** to recognize human faces. To make art, ADA uses its camera to look at someone's face. It then uses a pen to draw a portrait. ADA moves like a human artist. For example, it can pause and "look" at the person while it draws.

3   Ai-Da, another robot artist named after Ada Lovelace, actually looks like a human artist. Ai-Da uses cameras in its eyes to look at a person. Then the robot uses its bionic arm to draw a portrait. Each drawing is different. Ai-Da is programmed not to draw the exact same picture. This ability makes it more like a human artist. Ai-Da can also talk. Ai-Da can draw, but it can't paint. Instead, a human artist adds paint to its drawings. Art collectors have already spent over $1 million on Ai-Da's paintings.

4   Like ADA, e-David started life in a car factory. Two professors in Germany turned e-David into a robot artist. Unlike ADA, e-David doesn't draw live portraits. Instead, it takes a photo of someone with a camera. It then recreates the photo using paint. The robot uses a paint brush and 24 colors to **produce** its work. A computer tells e-David where to put the paint. The paintings look very much like the **original** photos. e-David has human qualities, too. For example, it can correct mistakes. e-David also signs its name on finished paintings.

5   In 2016, e-David, along with 24 other robot artists, participated in a **contest** called RobotArt. Organizers of RobotArt say the contest "combines art and engineering to enhance[3] both fields." A robot called Cloudpainter won the 2018 competition. One of Cloudpainter's paintings is of a person that the robot **imagined**. Some people think that robot artists like Cloudpainter aren't real artists. But it is clear that robot art is pushing both art and engineering forward.

Cloudpainter

---

[1]**sculpture** (n) a piece of art made out of wood, clay, metal, or stone.

[2]**drone** (n) an aircraft without a pilot

[3]**enhance** (v) to improve

B MAIN IDEAS Match paragraph number (2–5) next to a possible heading. Two headings are extra.

a. _____ Robots Teach Humans to Paint

b. _____ Get a Signed Copy of Your Favorite Painting

c. _____ Watch a Robot Draw Your Portrait

d. _____ Robots Show Off Their Work

e. _____ A Robot with Camera Eyes

f. _____ Robots Can't Paint

CRITICAL THINKING Assess features to form an opinion

When you compare features of people or things, you can see their strengths and weaknesses. This helps you to make an informed opinion of what you are comparing.

C DETAILS Check (✓) the features and abilities that are mentioned in the article about each robot.

Features and abilities	ADA	Ai-Da	e-David
1. can paint			
2. has cameras			
3. sells artwork			
4. was an industrial robot			
5. signs paintings			
6. can talk			
7. competes in art contests			

REFLECT   Assess robot art.

Write answers to the questions. Then discuss your ideas in a small group.

1. What is your opinion of Cloudpainter's painting?

_____

2. Do you think robot art is a good use of technology? Explain.

_____

3. Do you think art by a robot should cost the same, less, or more than art by a human?

_____

WRITE

UNIT TASK Write a paragraph about a graph.

You are going to write a paragraph about a graph. You will describe its main features. Use the ideas, vocabulary, and skills from the unit.

A MODEL Read the paragraph. Then look at the line graph and write the numbers from the model in the correct places.

Sales of Robots

The graph shows the sales of industrial and non-industrial robots from 2015 to the present. The graph includes sales for robots used in factories and robots used in places like hospitals and stores. According to the graph, sales of both kinds of robots have increased since 2015. Sales of industrial robots have increased by nearly 100% since 2015. Factories bought about [1]$1 billion of industrial robots in 2015 and [2]$2 billion in 2019. Sales of non-industrial robots, however, have risen even faster over the past few years. [3]In 2015, companies invested in over $1.5 billion worth of non-industrial robots. That number reached [4]about $3 billion in 2016. Now, [5]non-industrial robot sales are about $6.5 million. Clearly there is more demand for non-industrial robots.

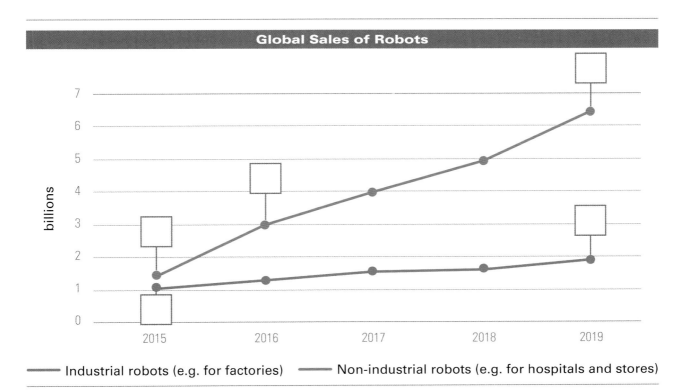

Global Sales of Robots

Industrial robots (e.g. for factories) Non-industrial robots (e.g. for hospitals and stores)

B ANALYZE THE MODEL Complete the outline of the model paragraph.

Title: _____.

What the graph shows: The graph shows _____

_____.

Main point: According to the graph, sales for _____

_____.

Supporting idea 1: Sales of industrial robots _____

_____.

    Detail: _____

Supporting idea 2: Sales of non-industrial robots, however, _____

_____.

    Details: _____

_____

_____

Concluding sentence: _____

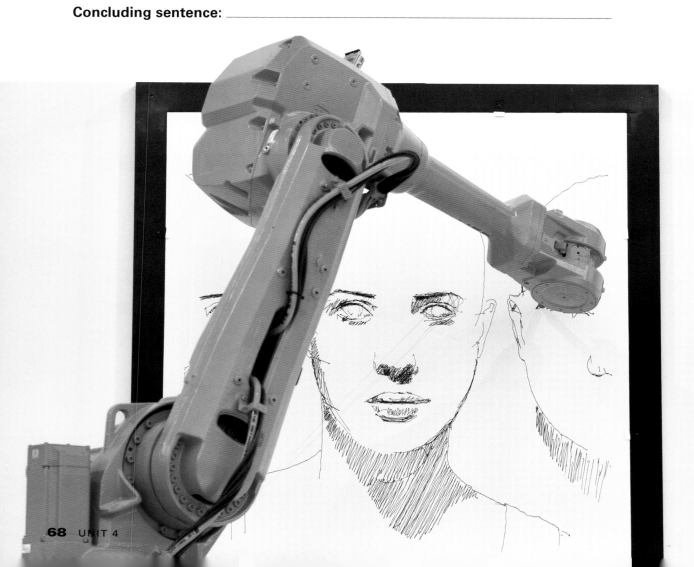

GRAMMAR Simple past and present perfect

We use the **simple past** to describe an event or time period that is completed.

> *Between 2005 and 2018, STEM jobs **grew** from about 6.4 million to almost 8 million.*
>
> *Jobs in computer science **increased** 100 percent last year.*

We use the **present perfect** to talk about things that started in the past and continue today.

> *STEM jobs **have grown** steadily for the past several years.*
>
> *Jobs in computer science **have increased** almost 100 percent each year since 2011.*

To form the present perfect, use *have* or *has (not)* + the past participle of a verb.

> *Sales **have remained** the same for the past five years. They **have not risen**.*
>
> *The rate **has risen** and **fallen** several times since 2016.*

We often use these time words and phrases with the present perfect:

> *for several years   since 2000   over the years   lately   already   yet*

Note: See the appendices for a list of common irregular past and past participle verb forms.

C GRAMMAR Find and underline the simple past and present perfect verbs in the model paragraph.

D GRAMMAR Complete each sentence with the simple past or present perfect of the verb.

1. Sales _____ (increase) 20 percent in the last three years.

2. According to the graph, the company _____ (sell) 90 percent of their phones last year.

3. As the chart shows, jobs in this field _____ (decrease) since 2000.

4. The number of available jobs _____ (not/change) in the past two years.

5. China _____ (have) the largest number of STEM graduates in 2019.

6. The number of STEM graduates _____ (not/rise) as much as needed in the past few years.

7. The chart shows that production numbers _____ (stay) the same for several years.

8. Schools in this district _____ (offer) art classes to students last semester.

9. Art-related jobs in the state _____ (fall) lately.

10. Salaries in the STEM fields _____ (rise) 20 percent in 2020.

E GRAMMAR Write sentences using the correct form of the words and phrases. Use the simple past or present perfect.

1. Technology/change a lot/in the last 20 years

   _____.

2. Smartphones/advance a lot/since the early 2000s

   _____.

3. Computers/become necessary/for everyday life

   _____.

4. Art and technology/be/the stars of the 2018 RobotArt contest

   _____.

F EDIT Read the paragraph. Find and correct four errors with the present perfect.

Growth of Computer Science Students and Jobs

The line graph shows the number of jobs and students in the field of computer science from 2011 to the present. According to the graph, there are many more computing jobs than computer science students. The number of computer science students has increase quite a bit since 2011. In the last nine years, the number rose from 50,000 to nearly 400,000. However, the number of computer jobs has grown even more. The number gone from 150,000 to about 1.4 million. Since 2011 the number of computing jobs has growing much faster than the number of computer science students. Now there are nine times more computer science jobs than students. It's clear that there are a lot of computer science jobs available, and we need more computer science students.

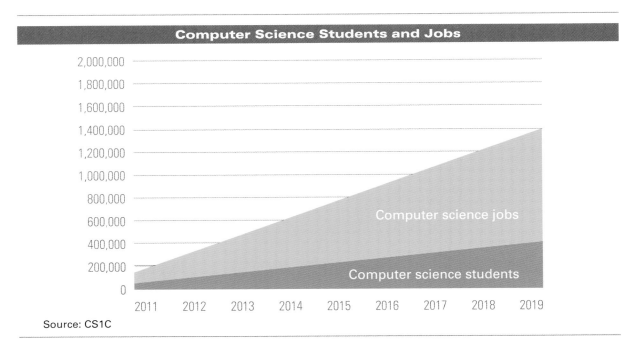

Source: CS1C

PLAN & WRITE

G PLAN You are going to write a summary of one of the graphs below. Choose one and answer these questions.

1. What kind of graph is it (a bar graph or a line graph)?

   _____

2. What is the main point of the graph? _____

   _____

3. What are some interesting details in the graph? _____

   _____

   _____

   _____

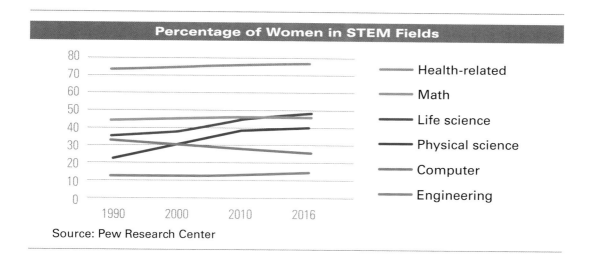

Source: Pew Research Center

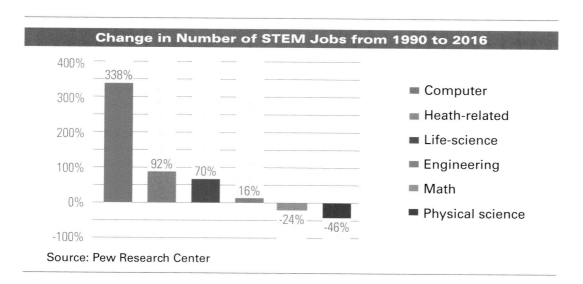

Source: Pew Research Center

WRITING SKILL Summarize charts and graphs

When you summarize a chart or a graph, begin by stating what it generally shows. For example:

The bar chart shows the number of tech jobs from 2009 to 2019.

Then add a topic sentence that states what the main trend or point is. For example:

According to the graph, tech jobs have increased over the past ten years.

After you introduce the main trend or point, provide supporting ideas about different parts of the graph. For example, describe the highest or lowest values. Finish your paragraph by writing a conclusion about the information.

H OUTLINE Complete the outline for your paragraph. Use your ideas from activity G.

Title: _____

What the graph shows: _____

Main point: _____ , _____

Supporting idea 1: _____

   Details: _____

Supporting idea 2: _____

   Details: _____

Concluding sentence: _____

I FIRST DRAFT Use your outline to write a first draft of your paragraph.

J REVISE Use this list as you write your second draft.

☐ Do you state what the graph generally shows?

☐ Do you have a topic sentence that gives the main point or trend of the graph?

☐ Do your supporting ideas give information about parts of the graph?

☐ Is there any information that doesn't belong?

K EDIT Use this list as you write your final draft.

☐ Did you use the simple past and present perfect correctly?

☐ Do your subjects and verbs agree?

☐ Did you spell all the words correctly?

☐ Did you use correct punctuation?

L FINAL DRAFT Reread your paragraph and correct any errors. Then submit it to your teacher.

REFLECT

A Check (✓) the Reflect activities you can do and the academic skills you can use.

☐ match skills to STEM jobs

☐ evaluate STEAM careers

☐ compare humans with technology

☐ assess robot art

☐ write a paragraph about a graph

☐ identify purpose and audience

☐ summarize charts and graphs

☐ simple past and present perfect

☐ assess features to form an opinion

B Write the vocabulary words from the unit in the correct place. Add any other words that you learned. Circle words you still need to practice.

NOUN	VERB	ADJECTIVE	ADVERB & OTHER

C Reflect on the ideas in the unit as you answer these questions.

1. How can students better prepare themselves for STEAM careers?

_____

_____

_____

2. What ideas or skills in this unit will be most useful to you in the future? Explain.

_____

_____

_____

WHY WE TRAVEL

A photographer catches
her son enjoying the ride.

CONNECT TO THE TOPIC

1. Why do people travel? What reason does the photo suggest?

2. Do you enjoy traveling? Explain.

WATCH

EXPEDITION TANZANIA

A student group poses with their hosts on a trip to Tanzania, Africa.

A PREDICT What do you think the students in the photo will do on their trip? Watch the video and check your prediction. ▶ 5.1

B Choose the correct answers. Watch the video again if necessary. ▶ 5.1

1. What was a main purpose of the trip?

   a. to take photos   b. to learn a new language   c. to work in a village

2. What is the main reason students said the trip was "life-changing"?

   a. They saw unique animals and learned to take beautiful photos.

   b. They laughed and danced and had a good time.

   c. They learned about a very different way of life from their own.

3. What did the students do with the Tanzanian people?

   a. They watched them sing and dance.

   b. They ate meals with them.

   c. They sang and danced with them.

C Have you had a life-changing trip? If yes, explain. If no, what kind of trip do you want to have?

PREPARE TO READ

A VOCABULARY Complete the sentences with the correct form of the words from the box. Use a dictionary if necessary.

impact (n)	lifetime (n)	mood (n)	reduce (v)	strengthen (v)
last (v)	measure (v)	opposite (n)	reward (v)	unexpected (adj)

1. Watching a funny TV show can improve your _____ when you are feeling unhappy.

2. Seeing the northern lights is the experience of a _____ for many people.

3. You can _____ your legs if you ride a bike ride a few times a week.

4. Canned food _____ a long time and doesn't need refrigeration, so it's perfect for camping.

5. In a study, scientists _____ how happy people were after going on a trip. They found that people were much happier.

6. Spending time in the community can have a positive _____ on your health.

7. You can't plan for everything when you travel. _____ situations like lost luggage can occur.

8. The _____ of feeling happy is feeling sad.

9. Flying can make people nervous. To _____ this feeling, they could listen to music.

10. A company often _____ its workers with more vacation days after five years of work.

B PERSONALIZE Discuss these questions with a partner.

1. What do you do to feel better when you are in a bad **mood**?

2. What **unexpected** situations have you, or someone you know, had during a trip?

REFLECT Consider reasons to travel.

Study the pie chart. Write answers to the questions. Then discuss them with a partner.

1. Why do most people travel, according to the chart? _____

2. What is the least common reason people travel? _____

3. Why do you like to travel? Choose three reasons from the chart. _____

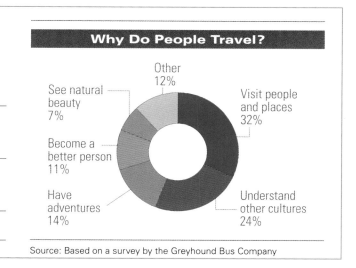

Why Do People Travel?

- Other 12%
- See natural beauty 7%
- Become a better person 11%
- Have adventures 14%
- Visit people and places 32%
- Understand other cultures 24%

Source: Based on a survey by the Greyhound Bus Company

READ

A PREVIEW Skim the article. Why do you think the writer wrote it?

   a. To describe a great trip people should take

   b. To explain the advantages of taking trips

   c. To summarize the steps people should take to have a better trip

B MAIN IDEAS Read the article carefully. Then match the paragraph number (2–4) with its main idea. Two ideas are extra.

   a. ____ Travel is good for the economy.

   b. ____ Travel can improve a person's career.

   c. ____ Travel has positive effects on physical health.

   d. ____ Travel improves our mental health.

   e. ____ Travel is a fun experience.

C DETAILS Read the statements. Write T for *True*, F for *False*, and NG for *Not Given*.

   1. ____ Women who travel have fewer heart problems.

   2. ____ Middle-aged men are more likely to have heart attacks.

   3. ____ Planning a trip does not make people happy.

   4. ____ Taking a short trip can reduce stress levels.

   5. ____ Not taking a vacation helps you get more done at work.

   6. ____ Managers can get promoted when they take vacations.

CRITICAL THINKING Evaluate ideas

As you read any text, **evaluate** the writer's ideas. They may not be correct. Are the ideas supported with enough evidence? Not everything in print is factual or well-supported. Evaluating what you read helps you be a more critical thinker and reader.

SURPRISING BENEFITS OF TRAVEL

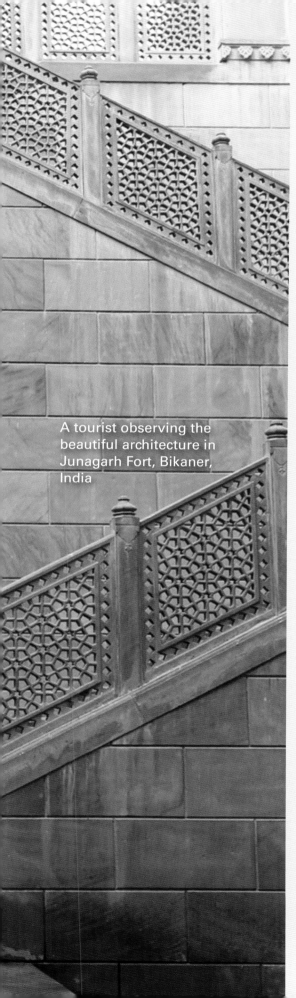

A tourist observing the beautiful architecture in Junagarh Fort, Bikaner, India

1   Traveling is fun. When we travel, we see new places. We have new experiences. And it's often better than our everyday routines. Traveling can also have some **unexpected** benefits that help us have better lives.

HEART HEALTHY

2   First of all, traveling can help you live longer. One study proves this. The study compared two groups of women. One group traveled at least twice a year. The other group traveled once every six years. The first group had a much lower risk of heart disease, the study found. The results are similar for men. Researchers at the State University of New York looked at the health of a group of middle-aged men. They found that taking a vacation once a year **reduced** the men's risk of heart disease by thirty percent.

FEELING GOOD...FOR LONGER

3   Being on vacation makes us happy. But researchers in Austria found something surprising: This happiness **lasts** a long time. They **measured** the stress levels[1] of 40 managers. Then they told the managers to take a short vacation. After the managers came home, the researchers measured their stress levels again. The managers' stress levels were, of course, much lower. The researchers kept measuring every day. They found that the managers continued to have lower stress levels. In fact, they still felt good six weeks after their vacations. Other research suggests that just *planning* a trip can improve your **mood**. A 2014 study showed that people feel less stressed just thinking about possible trips. They feel happy even if those trips don't really happen. In other words, people feel good weeks before and weeks after taking a vacation.

TAKE A VACATION, GET AHEAD

4   Traveling can have a positive **impact** at work, too. Many workers worry that going on vacation will affect their careers. They feel they must work all the time to keep their job. However, studies show that the **opposite** is true. Workers who go on vacation usually come back happier. And according to the book *The Happiness Advantage*, a happy brain is over 30% more productive. Managers like productive workers. They often **reward** them. In fact, workers who take vacations are 6.5% more likely to get a promotion[2], according to one report. So, getting away from work can actually help your career.

5   Traveling isn't only fun. It's also a way to **strengthen** your body and your mind. A trip may last only a few days or weeks, but the benefits may last a **lifetime**.

---

[1]**level** (n) the amount of something (e.g., stress)

[2]**promotion** (n) a move to a better job or position

READING SKILL Understand pronoun reference

Pronouns take the place of nouns and noun phrases that appear somewhere else in the same sentence or in a previous sentence. It's important to understand which noun or noun phrase each pronoun refers to.

> I love **traveling**. **It** makes me happy.
> **Planning a trip** helps **some people**. For example, **it** can make **them** happy.

Pronouns match the nouns that they refer to in gender (*he, she*) and in number.

> **Jaime** loves to travel. **He** takes five trips a year.

We often use *they* and *them* to refer to a single person when the person's gender isn't given.

> When a **person** travels, **they** often see things in a new way. Travelling helps **them** see the world differently.

D APPLY Answer the questions about the reading.

1. What does *they* refer to in line 7 of paragraph 2? _____

2. What do *they* and *their* refer to in line 8 of paragraph 3? _____

3. What does *them* refer to in line 7 of paragraph 4? _____

4. What does *it* refer to in line 1 of paragraph 5? _____

REFLECT   Describe types of vacations.

Use the adjectives or your own ideas to write a sentence that describes each trip. In a small group, say which trip you want to go on and why.

| fun | relaxing | educational | scary | boring | exhausting | risky | inspiring |

▶ a week on a beach
▶ a sightseeing weekend in Paris
▶ visiting museums for a day

▶ a two-week cruise
▶ a week hiking in the mountains
▶ a week doing extreme sports

1. _____
2. _____
3. _____
4. _____
5. _____
6. _____

PREPARE TO READ

A VOCABULARY Complete the sentences with the correct form of the words from the box. Use a dictionary if necessary.

allow (v)	deeply (adv)	host (n)	involve (v)	popularity (n)
citizen (n)	expose (v)	interact (v)	organize (v)	relax (v)

1. Machu Picchu has increased in _____ over the years. The Peruvian government limits the number of tourists now.

2. Many people are _____ concerned about global warming. They believe it is one of the biggest problems we face.

3. Learning the language _____ you to get more out of a visit to a new country.

4. If you _____ with local people in stores or cafes, you can practice speaking their language.

5. A _____ of the world is a person who feels as though they can live in any country or culture.

6. A successful trip _____ a lot of preparation. You need to figure out airplane tickets, hotels, and car rentals.

7. You can reserve your own flights and hotels, or you can have a travel company _____ your trip.

8. Traveling _____ people to new experiences and shows them different ways of living.

9. If you want to _____ on vacation, sit on a warm beach and read a book.

10. Polite guests bring their _____ a gift from home as a thank-you.

REFLECT Evaluate vacation activities.

You are going to read about a new kind of travel. Look at the list of activities below. Check (✓) the one(s) you would like to do on a vacation. Then discuss your reasons with a partner.

☐ learn the local language

☐ stay with a local family

☐ make crafts with local artists

☐ volunteer at a local farm

☐ take classes at a local college

☐ cook a meal with a local family

TRAVEL
LIKE A LOCAL

A fishing boat opens a net to catch fish in the sea near Phu Yen Province, Vietnam.

A PREVIEW Read the title. Then skim the blog post. What do you think it's mainly about?

a. How Vietnam attracts experiential travelers

b. Why experiential travel is becoming more popular

c. Where to be an experiential tourist in your town

1   What is your perfect vacation? Popular trips include **relaxing** on a warm beach. Or they **involve** sightseeing in a beautiful city. Increasingly, though, many of us don't want to just visit a place. We want to experience it.

2   Experiential[1] travel **allows** travelers to get closer to local people and their culture. For example, experiential travelers might stay a few weeks with local **hosts**. They might take classes to learn a local craft. They might volunteer at local businesses, such as farms or restaurants. In other words, these travelers immerse[2] themselves in a different culture. According to TripAdvisor, experiential trips have grown over 40% since 2015. The **popularity** of experiential travel shows no sign of slowing.

3   Mejdi Tours is one example of an experiential travel company. Mejdi **organizes** experiential trips to different parts of the world. Their goal is to create trips where both local people and travelers benefit. One such trip is in Vietnam. There, a tour guide goes with a small group of travelers to meet with a local fisherman. They learn how to fix nets and throw them in the water. They catch fish together. Afterwards they all cook and eat a meal with the fisherman's family.

4   Experiential travel helps people become better **citizens.** First of all, it lets them understand a place more **deeply** than tourists usually do. As one traveler says, traditional travel is "like studying science without ever doing a scientific experiment." Since they often stay and work in one place, travelers learn more about the lives of local people.

It **exposes** them to different ways of living and working. Experiential travelers often make life-long friends with local people. They stay in touch[3] after the trip has finished. Experiential travel helps travelers—and local people—feel like they are part of a global community.

5   You don't need to use a travel company to get the benefits of experiential travel. You can do it by yourself. You can ask local people questions when you travel. Ask a driver about her life. Ask the hotel receptionist about his story. You can also take a cooking class or join a soccer game in the street. Listening to people's stories and **interacting** with local people will change your understanding of the place you are visiting.

COMMENTS (2)

👤 **Abdul**

Nice article! Last year I went on a walking tour of London. Our guide was actually a homeless man. We learned so much about the city!

👤 **Kamila**

I'm thinking about going to Japan next year. I want to meditate[4] at a Buddhist Temple. I think it will be really inspiring!

---

[1]**experiential** (adj) based on experience

[2]**immerse** (v) to involve yourself in an activity

[3]**stay in touch** (v phr) to continue to communicate by writing or calling

[4]**meditate** (v) to focus the mind, for spiritual purposes or to relax

---

B MAIN IDEAS Match the paragraph number (2–5) to the main idea. Two ideas are extra.

Experiential travelers…

a. _____ usually go to Vietnam.

b. _____ can take organized trips.

c. _____ are going on more vacations.

d. _____ immerse themselves in a new place.

e. _____ understand the world better.

f. _____ can get benefits traveling on their own.

C DETAILS Complete the concept map about the benefits of experiential travel. Use one word for each answer.

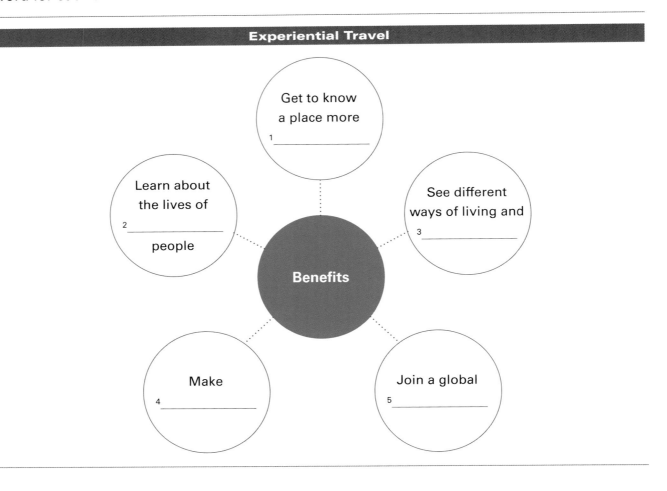

Experiential Travel

Get to know a place more
1 _____

Learn about the lives of
2 _____
people

See different ways of living and
3 _____

Benefits

Make
4 _____

Join a global
5 _____

D Read the sentences from the blog. Write the word(s) that each bold pronoun refers to.

1. Increasingly, though, many of us don't want to just visit a place: We want to experience **it**.

   it: _____

2. There, a tour guide goes with a small group of travelers to meet with a local fisherman. **They** learn how to fix nets and throw **them** in the water.

   They: _____   **them:** _____

3. Since **they** often stay and work in one place, travelers learn more about the lives of local people.

   they: _____

REFLECT   Plan an experiential trip in your town.

Think of an experiential trip someone could take in your town or city. In your notebook, write the location of the trip, and the activities visitors could do. Then share your trip with a partner.

WRITE

Hikers on the path to the Kumano Hongu Taisha Grand Shrine in Wakayama Prefecture, Japan

UNIT TASK Write a paragraph about a trip.

You are going to write a short report about a trip and why it is interesting. Use the ideas, skills, and vocabulary from this unit.

A MODEL Read the paragraph. Would you like to go on this trip? Explain your answer to a partner.

A Hiking Tour from Kyoto to Tokyo

A hiking tour in Japan is a popular experiential trip for several reasons. One reason is that it's a good way to learn about some of Japan's history. This hike goes from the old capital of Japan, Kyoto, to the current capital, Tokyo. This route was an important link between the two cities for over a thousand years. You learn all about this link, so you'll understand more about the history of Japan. Another reason is that it's great exercise. You walk over 15 miles every day for 11 days. You also hike over mountains and through forests. Finally, the most important reason is that this trip is very relaxing. Since it is different from your regular routine, you forget all about the stresses of daily life. It is also relaxing because the tour includes hot spring baths in various places. The hiking tour from Kyoto to Tokyo is a great trip because it's educational, healthy, and relaxing all at the same time.

B ANALYZE THE MODEL Complete the tasks.

1. Write the topic and the controlling idea.

   Topic: _____

   Controlling idea: _____

2. Write the three main reasons the writer likes the walking tour.

   _____

   _____

   _____

3. Write three details the writer gives that are facts.

   _____

   _____

   _____

WRITING SKILL Write a concluding sentence

The last sentence in a paragraph is usually the concluding sentence. A concluding sentence tells the reader that you have finished explaining your main idea. To conclude a paragraph, you can do one of the following.

▸ **Restate the main idea** using different words.
   In summary, travel has physical, emotional, and mental benefits.

▸ **Give an opinion.**
   I believe that experiential travel is better for travelers and locals.

▸ **Make a prediction.**
   You will understand Vietnam better if you take the Mekong River tour.

▸ **Make a suggestion.**
   If you want a relaxing vacation, I suggest you take a hot springs tour of Japan.

C APPLY Underline the concluding sentence in the model paragraph. What does it do?

a. Restates the main idea

b. Gives an opinion

c. Gives a suggestion

D APPLY Write three different concluding sentences for the model paragraph.

1. (opinion) _____

_____

2. (prediction) _____

_____

3. (suggestion) _____

_____

E APPLY Choose the concluding sentence that best restates the main idea.

Topic sentence: A volunteer work trip is a great way to travel because you get job experience, you learn about the local culture, and you help people.

a. When you volunteer in a new country, you learn about the people and the culture.

b. A volunteer work trip is a great idea because you get job experience, you help people, and you learn a lot about the culture.

c. Improving work skills and helping others while you learn about a new place is a great way to travel.

GRAMMAR Connecting words for reasons and results

We use *because* or *since* to introduce a reason. ***Because/since* + subject + verb** forms an **adverb clause of reason**. An adverb clause is a dependent clause. It can come before or after the main clause. When it comes first, use a comma.

*Experiential travelers learn more about a place **because** <u>they stay with local people</u>.*
reason

***Since** <u>they stay with local people</u>, experiential travelers learn more about a place.*
reason

We use *so* to introduce a result. *So* connects two independent clauses.

*Travelers stay with local people, **so** <u>they learn more about a place</u>.*
result

F GRAMMAR Find and circle the four connecting words for reasons and results in the model paragraph. Underline the reasons or results that follow them.

G GRAMMAR Choose the correct word to complete the sentences. Add commas where needed.

1. **Because / So** I want to improve my Portuguese I'm traveling around Brazil for three months.

2. Rafael went to Chichen Itza in Mexico **so / because** he wanted to learn about Mayan culture.

3. Some people are worried about climate change **since / so** they only travel by train or ship.

4. Cycling tours in France are popular **since / so** many people enjoy seeing beautiful views while they exercise.

5. The weather is usually hot and sunny in the summer **because / so** hotels are often fully booked.

6. **So / Since** popular tourist destinations can be crowded it's a good idea to visit less-popular destinations.

H GRAMMAR Connect the sentence parts using *because, since,* or *so*. More than one answer may be possible.

1. Sonya loves to cook. She's taking a food tour of Italy next year.
   (*so*)

   _____

   _____

2. Ana is interested in Vietnam. She's going to stay on a Vietnamese farm.
   (*because*)

   _____

   _____

3. Chuy wants to get a lot of exercise. He's going on a hiking tour in Peru.
   (*since*)

   _____

   _____

4. Mona is visiting Beijing for the weekend. She loves walking around the old palaces.
   (because)

   _____

   _____

A woman carries a bale of hay on a goat farm in Spain.

I **EDIT** Find and correct four errors with connecting words for reasons and results.

A Working Vacation in Spain

A working trip on an organic farm in Spain is a great adventure for many reasons. First of all, you live with a farming family so you learn a lot about the local culture. You see how they live, what they eat, and what they do for fun. It's also an excellent way to improve your Spanish. Because, you work all day with local people you have to use Spanish to communicate. Another reason that this is a great trip is that it's good for your health. Farming is physically hard, because you get plenty of exercise every day. A work stay on a Spanish farm is an excellent way to learn about a culture, improve your language skills, and come home in great shape!

PLAN & WRITE

J **BRAINSTORM** Think of two interesting trips. They could be vacations you have taken or experiential trips you know about. Then write four reasons why people go on each trip.

Trips	Reasons to go

You can also **introduce reasons** with phrases like:

The main reason is…

One reason is…

A more important reason is…

K OUTLINE Choose the trip that interests you the most and complete the outline for your paragraph.

Title: _____

Topic sentence: _____ .

Supporting idea 1: One reason _____ .

    Details: _____

    _____

Supporting idea 2: Another reason _____ .

    Details: _____

    _____

Supporting idea 3: Finally, the most important reason _____ .

    Details: _____

    _____

Concluding sentence: _____ .

L FIRST DRAFT Use your outline to write a first draft of your paragraph.

M REVISE Use this list as you write your second draft.

☐ Does your topic sentence introduce the main idea of your paragraph?

☐ Do your detail sentences give more information about each supporting idea?

☐ Does the paragraph have a concluding sentence?

☐ Is there any information that doesn't belong?

N EDIT Use this list as you write your final draft.

☐ Did you use connecting words for reasons and results correctly?

☐ Do your subjects and verbs agree?

☐ Did you spell all the words correctly?

☐ Did you use correct punctuation?

O FINAL DRAFT Read your essay and correct any errors. Then submit it to your teacher.

REFLECT

A Check (✓) the Reflect activities you can do and the academic skills you can use.

☐ consider reasons to travel

☐ describe types of vacations

☐ evaluate vacation activities

☐ plan an experiential trip in your town

☐ write a paragraph about a trip

☐ understand pronoun reference

☐ write a concluding sentence

☐ connecting words for reasons and results

☐ evaluate ideas

B Write the vocabulary words from the unit in the correct place. Add any other words that you learned. Circle words you still need to practice.

NOUN	VERB	ADJECTIVE	ADVERB & OTHER

C Reflect on the ideas in the unit as you answer these questions.

1. Where do you want to travel to in the future?

_____

_____

_____

2. What ideas or skills in this unit will be most useful to you in the future?

_____

_____

_____

THE MYSTERY OF DREAMS

Max Richter performs "Sleep" at the Bass Concert Hall in Austin, Texas. People rest or sleep as they listen.

CONNECT TO THE TOPIC

1. What type of music do you think "Sleep" is?

2. How are your dreams similar to reality? How are they different?

93

WATCH

WHAT DOES AN ASTRONAUT DREAM ABOUT?

The International
Space Station

A Watch the video. Then write T for *True* or F for *False*. ▶ 6.1

In her dream, Helen Sharman...

1. _____ is on a spaceship.

2. _____ moves quickly.

3. _____ looks out of a window.

4. _____ sees the Earth.

5. _____ sees stars.

6. _____ is alone.

7. _____ feels warm.

8. _____ wants to return to Earth.

British astronaut
Helen Sharman

B How did Sharman feel when her dream ended? Why did she feel this way?
Discuss your ideas with a partner.

C Write answers to the questions in your notebook. Then share your answers
with a partner.

1. What dream have you had more than once? Describe the dream.

2. How do you usually feel when you wake up after that dream? Happy?
Relieved?

94 UNIT 6

PREPARE TO READ

A VOCABULARY Read the defintions. Then complete the sentences with the correct form of the words.

actual (adj) real
extremely (adv) very
participant (n) a person in an activity
process (v) to deal with
separate (v) to divide
signal (n) an action that sends a message
stage (n) a particular time in an event
theory (n) an idea about why something happens
therapy (n) a form of treatment that helps people with problems
upsetting (adj) causing feelings of sadness or worry

1. Scientists have many different _____ about why we dream.

2. Some think that dreams are a form of _____. They help people deal with difficult situations in their lives.

3. Sometimes when I first wake up, it is hard to _____ dreams from real life.

4. Some think that dreams help us _____ ideas so that we wake up with a solution.

5. The students were _____ in a sleep study. They said that it was _____ difficult to fall asleep in a lab.

6. The _____ meaning of a dream is not always clear. While some dreams seem _____, they might have a positive meaning.

7. There are several _____ of sleep, but we don't dream in all of them.

8. Cells in our brains send _____ to other cells, causing dreams.

REFLECT   Analyze why we dream.

You are going to read about the reasons we dream. Why do you think we dream? Check (✓) the reasons below. Then share your ideas with a group.

Dreams...

_____ help us process memories.

_____ improve our emotions.

_____ have no meaning or purpose.

_____ keep our brains busy while we sleep.

_____ solve problems we have in real life.

_____ make us more creative.

READ

A PREVIEW Skim the article. Does it give a single answer to the question in the title or does it offer different theories? Tell a partner. Then read the article.

B MAIN IDEAS Read the statements. Write T for *True*, F for *False*, and NG for *Not Given*.

1. _____ Scientists agree on a theory about why we dream.

2. _____ We only dream during REM sleep.

3. _____ Dreaming can help us with emotional events in our lives.

4. _____ Dreaming is a kind of therapy, according to Walker's study.

5. _____ Missing non-REM sleep makes us sick.

Two explorers rest with their sled dog on the sea ice in Ellesmere Island, Canada.

WHY DO WE DREAM?

6.1

1   From the ancient Greeks to modern-day bloggers, people have always been interested in dreams. Some scientists believe that dreams are the result of random[1] electrical **signals** in the brain. To them, dreams have no real meaning. Other scientists think that dreaming lets us combine new memories with old ones. Whatever the reasons are, dreaming seems to be good for us.

2   Most of our dreams happen during REM[2] sleep, one of four main **stages** of sleep. Each instance of REM sleep lasts from ten minutes to an hour in adults. It is the time our brains are most active during sleep. Scientists think that we have five or more dreams at this time. REM sleep is ruled by the amygdala—the part of the brain that controls our most basic emotions. These include fear, joy, and love. This may explain why so many of our dreams can be scary, fun, and **extremely** strange.

3   Dreams are entertaining, but they could also be doing something useful. They might help us **process** emotionally painful memories. In a recent study in the United States, two groups of 17 adults looked at 150 photos. Some of the photos were **upsetting**. For example, some photos showed people badly hurt in car accidents. The first group looked at the photos once before sleeping and again after they woke up. The second group also looked at the photos

twice but didn't sleep between viewings. Matthew Walker, leader of the study, used an MRI machine to scan[3] the **participants'** brains. The scans showed that activity in the amygdala decreased for the participants in the first group. These people were less upset looking at the photos again. Walker thinks that dreaming made the photos less upsetting.

4   Walker's **theory** is that our brains "flag" upsetting events. These flags tell our brains to process these events while we are sleeping. When we dream, the brain **separates** the emotions from the event. Walker calls this "overnight **therapy**." The results of Walker's study show that dreaming may help us deal with **actual** upsetting events in our lives.

5   Whatever the purpose of dreaming is, not being able to dream is bad for us. In a study, people were woken up just as they were entering REM sleep. As a result, they developed a number of health issues such as depression and weight gain. As Matthew Walker suggests, "It's not time that heals all wounds[4]—it's REM sleep."

---

[1]**random** (adj) happening at any time for no reason

[2]**REM** (abbr) Rapid Eye Movement, a stage of sleep

[3]**scan** (v) to examine for problems or patterns

[4]**time heals all wounds** an expression meaning that feelings of sadness go away with time

READING SKILL Scan for specific information

When you need to find types of information (a keyword, name, or number), it's helpful to quickly scan the text. For example, if you need to find a year, look for a four-digit number. If you need to find someone's name, look for capitalized words. When you find a keyword, name, or number, read the sentences around it to understand the context. This will help you decide if you have found the correct information.

C APPLY Read the questions below. Choose the correct type of information to scan for. Then scan the article for the information and write the answers.

1. Where was the dream study done?   a. keyword   b. name   c. number

   _____

2. How many people participated?   a. keyword   b. name   c. number

   _____

3. Who was the lead scientist?   a. keyword   b. name   c. number

   _____

4. What machine was used?   a. keyword   b. name   c. number

   _____

5. What was the scientist's theory?   a. keyword   b. name   c. number

   _____

   _____

D DETAILS Number the events in the study in the correct order (1-5).

The researchers…

_____ showed the two groups the same pictures.

_____ noticed that the group who slept was less affected by the photos.

_____ divided the participants into two groups.

_____ concluded that dreaming may help us better deal with emotional events.

_____ scanned the participants' brains.

REFLECT   Assess research on dreams.

In the article, Matthew Walker calls dreams "overnight therapy." Do you agree? Do you think dreams help us deal with upsetting events in our lives? Write an answer in your notebook. Then discuss in a small group.

PREPARE TO READ

A VOCABULARY Write the correct word next to its definition. Use a dictionary if necessary.

accurate (adj)	base on (v phr)	face (v)	identify (v)	record (v)
alternatively (adv)	benefit (v)	frequently (adv)	image (n)	unique (adj)

1. _____: to take note of and store information

2. _____: often

3. _____: special; one-of-a-kind

4. _____: to deal with something difficult

5. _____: differently

6. _____: to be good for

7. _____: free from mistakes

8. _____: a picture

9. _____: to form an idea or opinion from specific information

10. _____: to recognize

B PERSONALIZE Discuss these questions with a partner.

1. How **frequently** do you remember your dreams? What kinds of things affect whether or not you remember your dreams?

2. What do you think your dreams are **based on**? Something you've been thinking about during the day? Memories? Something else?

3. Do you ever **record** your dreams? Explain.

REFLECT Consider the meaning of dreams.

You are going to read more about dreams. Look at the list of topics people often dream about. Check (✓) the ones you have dreamt about. What do you think these dreams mean? Discuss your ideas with a partner.

_____ flying   _____ being chased

_____ falling   _____ being late for a meeting or class

_____ losing teeth   _____ being lost

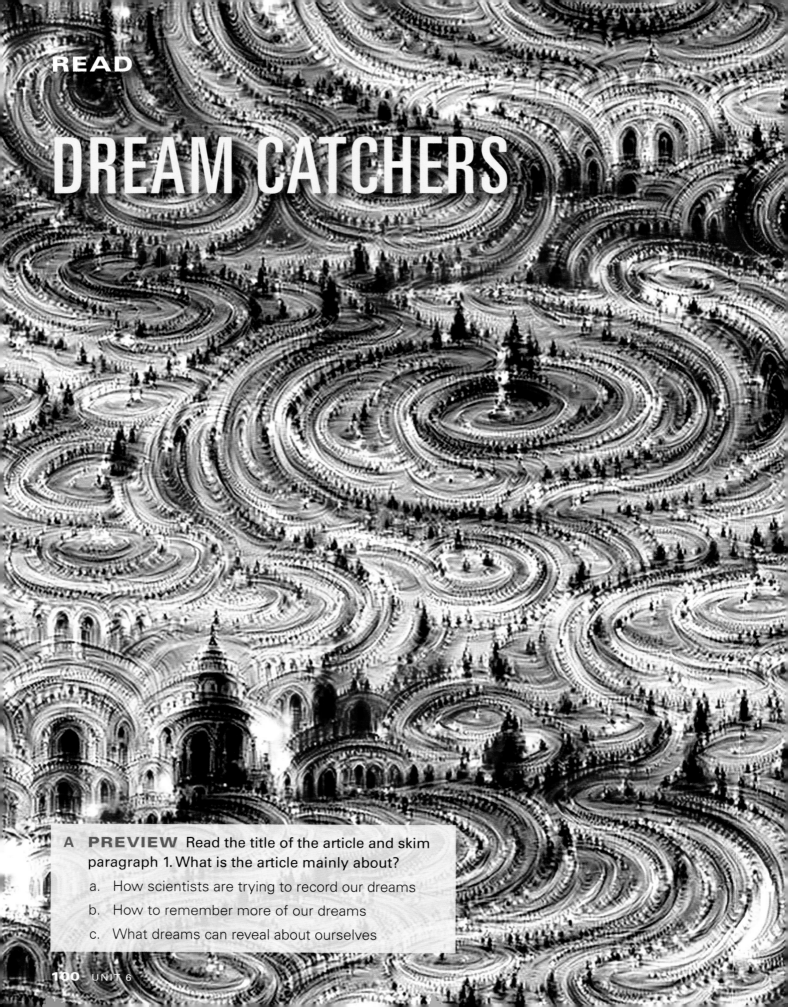

DREAM CATCHERS

A PREVIEW Read the title of the article and skim paragraph 1. What is the article mainly about?

a. How scientists are trying to record our dreams

b. How to remember more of our dreams

c. What dreams can reveal about ourselves

An image created by Google's DeepDream

1   Do you wish you could remember your dreams? Dreams are often difficult to remember and hard to describe. And most of us forget our dreams soon after we wake up. Some scientists, however, are learning how to **record** our dreams. Imagine one day waking up, turning on your TV, and watching a video of last night's dream.

2   Scientist Yukiyasu Kamitani recorded **images** from dreams. He realized that our dreams **frequently** include everyday objects like cars and houses. In 2013, Kamitani asked participants to look at hundreds of photos of these kinds of objects. As they looked at each object, he used an MRI machine to scan their brains. A computer then recorded their brain patterns[1]. Each object creates a **unique** pattern in the brain. Then, while the participants slept, Kamitani scanned their brains again. His computer tried to find the same patterns. It was seeing if they were dreaming about the objects. Kamitani reviewed the data from the computer. Then he created short videos **based on** the data. Afterwards, participants watched the videos. Surprisingly, they said the videos were about 70 percent **accurate**.

3   Other scientists have attempted to record speech in dreams. For example, in 2018, Daniel Oldis and David Schnyer asked participants to pronounce every sound in the English language. The researchers measured nerve signals[2] in participants' faces, throats, and lips as they spoke. Then, the participants were told to sleep. During REM sleep, Oldis and Schnyer measured the nerve signals again. When they found the same signals, they could **identify** what the participants likely said in their dreams.

4   But why would we want or need to watch our dreams? Sure, it might be entertaining to watch some of our more interesting dreams the next day or even years later. However, being aware of our dreams could **benefit** us in more important ways, too. Watching dreams might help us understand more about problems we **face** in our real lives. For example, if we dream about money night after night, we might want to pay more attention to our spending. It may be that we have money problems that we don't want to deal with in our waking life. Watching dreams may also make us more creative. Many great ideas such as songs, poems, and art have come from dreams.

5   Understanding our dreams might help us be better, healthier people. **Alternatively**, it might not. According to psychology professor Antonio Zadra, it's important "not to confuse dream experience with reality." Perhaps dreams are best forgotten.

---

[1]**pattern** (n) shape; form

[2]**nerve signals** (n phr) messages that nerves carry from the body to the brain

B MAIN IDEAS Complete the summary of the article with the correct form of the words.

| creativity | image | measure | problem | see | speech |

A scientist recorded what people ¹_____ in their dreams. He did this by recording their brain activity when they looked at ²_____. Other scientists recorded ³_____ from people's dreams. They ⁴_____ nerve signals in people's faces. Recording our dreams could help us in a few different ways. It could help us understand our real-life ⁵_____. It could also increase our ⁶_____.

C DETAILS Scan the article to find the two studies mentioned. Then answer the questions.

1. When did Yukiyasu Kamitani do his experiment? _____

2. What machine did he use to scan people's brains? _____

3. What were the names of the researchers who recorded speech in dreams?_____

4. When did they do their experiment? _____

D DETAILS Put the events in the correct order (1-6) on the timeline.

1. Kamitani reviewed the computer data.
2. A computer recorded brain patterns for each photo.
3. Participants said the videos were very accurate.
4. Participants slept while their brains were scanned again.
5. Kamitani showed participants photos and scanned their brains.
6. Kamitani made videos based on the data.

| | | | 1 | | |

REFLECT Respond to the idea of recording dreams.

How likely do you think it is that we will be able to record our dreams in the future? Explain your answer in a small group.

very likely   somewhat likely   somewhat unlikely   very unlikely

WRITE

A self-driving car, which allows you to relax while it drives for you

UNIT TASK Write an essay about the pros and cons of recording dreams.

You are going to write an essay for the following class assignment: "In the future we may be able to record our dreams. Discuss the advantages and disadvantages of being able to do this."

A MODEL Read the essay about the advantages and disadvantages of self-driving cars. Underline the main idea.

Sleeping while Driving?

Everyone is so busy these days, and not getting enough sleep is a real problem. One serious effect of this is falling asleep while driving. Self-driving cars might be a solution to this danger in the future. Car manufacturers think that in the future, we will sleep comfortably in our self-driving cars. However, having self-driving cars on the road could have both advantages and disadvantages.

On one hand, sleeping in our self-driving cars could make us safer and healthier. Tiredness is one of the major causes of car accidents. Self-driving cars will take control when a driver is too tired. This will probably mean fewer deaths on the road. In addition, some people think that self-driving cars will help people get more sleep. Over a third of us do not get enough sleep. This causes health problems. People with long commutes might get an hour or two extra sleep while their cars drive them to work.

On the other hand, self-driving cars might not be reliable. First, like any piece of equipment, self-driving cars might break down. The computer controlling a self-driving car could stop working and cause the car to stop suddenly. People asleep in the car could be hurt. Additionally, the car may make wrong turns or not know how to deal with a situation on the road. Some experts think it is probably better to have an awake driver at all times.

In conclusion, there are pros and cons for people sleeping in self-driving cars. They might help people who don't get enough sleep. Unfortunately, though, there are also serious safety concerns. Before you try a self-driving car, it is important to consider the advantages and disadvantages.

B ANALYZE THE MODEL Write the pros and cons from the model essay.

Pros of sleeping while driving	Cons of sleeping while driving
_____ _____	_____ _____

WRITING SKILL Expand a paragraph into an essay

Like a paragraph, an essay discusses one topic. However, an essay is longer—often four paragraphs or more. An essay follows the same basic organization as a paragraph—an introduction, supporting information, and a conclusion.

▶ The **introductory paragraph** includes a thesis statement, which states the main idea of the essay.

▶ Two or more **body paragraphs** give supporting information about the main idea. Each paragraph includes a topic sentence, supporting ideas, and details.

▶ The **concluding paragraph** includes a summary statement that restates the thesis statement using different words and/or a final thought about the topic.

C APPLY Complete the outline of the model essay.

Introductory paragraph
Thesis statement: Having self-driving cars on the road could have both advantages and disadvantages.

First body paragraph (pros)
Topic sentence: Sleeping in our self-driving cars could _____.

Supporting idea: Self-driving cars will take control when _____.

　Detail: _____

Supporting idea: Some people think that self-driving cars will help _____.

　Details: _____

Second body paragraph (cons)
Topic sentence: Self-driving cars might _____.

Supporting idea: Self-driving cars _____.

Details: _____

Supporting idea: Car could make wrong turns or _____.

Detail: _____

Concluding paragraph
Summary statement: In conclusion, there are pros and cons for sleeping in self-driving cars.

GRAMMAR Modals of possibility

You can use the modals *will*, *may*, *might*, and *could* to express possibility about the future. Use the base form of the verb after a modal.

Use *will* and *won't* to talk about things that you think are certain to happen.

> Scientists **will** study dreams in the future.
> They **won't** stop researching dreams.

Add *probably* to *will* if you are not completely certain, but it is likely.

> It **will probably** take a long time for scientists to record dreams.
> We **probably won't** be able to record our dreams in the next five years.

Use *may*, *may not*, *might*, *might not*, and *could* to talk about things that are less certain to happen. Note that we don't use *could not* to talk about the future.

> We **may** be able to record our dreams.
> Scientists **might not** find a way to record dreams.

D GRAMMAR Find and underline the modals of possibility in the body paragraphs of the model essay.

E GRAMMAR Read the sentences. How certain are the people making each statement? Write LC for *Less Certain*, L for *Likely*, and C for *Certain*.

1. _____ We will probably be able to watch our dreams in the future.

2. _____ We might never learn the purpose of dreams.

3. _____ Researchers might find a way to help us remember all of our dreams.

4. _____ People will continue to talk about dreams.

5. _____ People in the future could learn a lot about themselves by watching their own dreams.

6. _____ In my opinion, people won't want to record their dreams.

7. _____ Some participants might not be able to fall asleep in the lab.

8. _____ We'll probably never know the meaning of our dreams.

F GRAMMAR Complete each sentence with a modal of possibility. More than one answer is possible. Discuss your answers with a partner.

1. Researchers _____ learn more about why we dream.

2. We _____ be able to control our dreams.

3. Our dreams _____ play on our smartphones.

4. We _____ be able to remember all of our dreams.

5. People _____ want to record their own dreams.

6. Scientists _____ find out what causes dreams.

G GRAMMAR Complete the sentences with your own ideas about dream research. Use modals of possibility.

1. In the future, humans _____.

2. In ten years, humans probably _____.

3. In 50 years, people _____.

4. In 100 years, we _____.

5. By 2200, we probably _____.

H EDIT Read the introductory paragraph and first body paragraph of an essay. Find and correct six errors with modals of possibility.

An All-in-One Nutrition Drink

By 2050, there might be 10 billion people on planet Earth. This rapid growth means that we need to find a way to feed everyone without damaging our lands and seas. A drink that contains all of the protein, vitamins, and minerals that we need might be the answer. There are pros and cons of a meal-replacement drink that could to feed billions of people.

On one hand, a meal-replacement beverage would be convenient. People could saving time because they won't need to cook and clean. They will able to simply open a bottle and drink a complete meal. In addition, people might are healthier than they are now. Right now, people eat a lot of junk food and fast food. With a meal-replacement drink, they will getting important nutrients quickly and easily.

PLAN & WRITE

I **BRAINSTORM** Brainstorm the pros and cons of recording your dreams. Complete the chart with the ideas (a-i). Add your own ideas.

a. interesting–we can see what our brains are doing while we sleep

b. embarrassing

c. we might pay too much attention to dreams and what they mean

d. lose privacy—hackers could steal our dreams and show them online

e. fun—we can show other people

f. expensive to do

g. might help us understand ourselves, be more creative

h. might help us solve our problems

i. we might confuse dreams with reality

Pros	Cons

A young man participating in a sleep study

J OUTLINE Complete the outline for your essay. Use the two strongest pros and cons from your brainstorming.

Introductory paragraph

Thesis statement: *There could be both advantages and disadvantages to recording dreams.* .

First body paragraph (pros)

Topic sentence: On one hand, _____.

Supporting idea: _____.

    Details: _____

Supporting idea: In addition, _____.

    Details: _____

Second body paragraph (cons)

Topic sentence: On the other hand, _____.

Supporting idea: First, _____.

    Details: _____

Supporting idea: Additionally, _____.

    Details: _____

Concluding paragraph

Summary statement: *In conclusion, there are pros and cons of recording dreams.* .

K FIRST DRAFT Use your outline to write a first draft of your essay.

L REVISE Use this list as you write your second draft.
- ☐ Does your thesis statement introduce the main idea of your essay?
- ☐ Do your topic sentences support the thesis statement?
- ☐ Do you have a body paragraph with the pros and one with the cons?
- ☐ Do you include supporting ideas in each body paragraph?
- ☐ Is there any information that doesn't belong?

M EDIT Use this list as you write your final draft.
- ☐ Did you use modals correctly?
- ☐ Do your subjects and verbs agree?
- ☐ Did you spell all the words correctly?
- ☐ Did you use correct punctuation?

N FINAL DRAFT Reread your essay and correct any errors. Then submit it to your teacher.

REFLECT

A Check (✓) the Reflect tasks you can do and the academic skills you can use.

- ☐ analyze why we dream
- ☐ assess research on dreams
- ☐ consider the meaning of dreams
- ☐ respond to the idea of recording dreams
- ☐ write about the pros and cons of recording dreams

- ☐ scan for specific information
- ☐ expand a paragraph into an essay
- ☐ modals of possibility
- ☐ analyze pros and cons

B Write the vocabulary words from the unit in the correct place. Add any other words that you learned. Circle words you still need to practice.

NOUN	VERB	ADJECTIVE	ADVERB & OTHER

C Reflect on the ideas in the unit as you answer these questions.

1. If you could record your dreams, how could you use that ability to help you?

_____

_____

_____

2. What ideas or skills in this unit will be most useful to you in the future?

_____

_____

_____

CREATIVITY AT WORK

Designers in Mumbai, India, create taxi fabrics that tell stories about their city.

CONNECT TO THE TOPIC

1. What examples of creativity do you see in the photo?

2. How do you define creativity?

WHAT WILL YOU WEAR **TO CHANGE THE WORLD?**

A Read the ideas from the video. Then watch the video and check each idea as you hear it. ▶ 7.1

An idea for wearable technology that...

1. ✓ monitors your diet.
2. ____ walks for you.
3. ____ points you in the right direction.

4. ____ tells you when a robber is coming.
5. ____ monitors blood pressure and heart rate.
6. ____ lets you feel close to someone far away.

B How will each idea change the world? Match the ideas from activity A (1–6) to the solutions (a-f). Watch the video again if necessary.

The idea helps you...

a. ____ protect a disabled person.
b. ____ communicate with a friend.
c. ____ not get lost.

d. ____ stop feeling tired when walking.
e. ____ stay safe from bad people.
f. __1__ have a healthy weight.

C Which idea from the video would change your world the most? Discuss with a partner.

A woman brainstorms ideas for a competition to find the next best wearable technology.

PREPARE TO READ

A VOCABULARY Complete the sentences with the correct form of the words. Use a dictionary if necessary.

aim (v)	complain (v)	employee (n)	hire (v)	think of (v phr)
analyze (v)	data (n)	experiment (v)	solve (v)	value (v)

1. When companies want to _____ someone, they often advertise the job online.

2. For many people, the first iPhone _____ the problem of needing to carry a phone, a music player, and a camera separately.

3. When you _____ a good idea, write it down before you forget it.

4. Most companies _____ to increase sales from year to year.

5. Ice-cream companies often _____ with new flavors to increase sales.

6. It is important to _____ customer needs before opening a new business.

7. My boss _____ creativity in the people she works with.

8. _____ at Google get free food and gym classes.

9. Your smartphone keeps a lot of _____ about you, such as the websites you've visited.

10. When customers _____ about something that makes them unhappy, it is often best to just listen to them.

B PERSONALIZE Discuss your answers to the questions with a partner.

1. What do you **aim** to achieve by the end of this year?

2. What are things at work or school that you sometimes **complain** about?

3. What do you **value** in a friend or co-worker?

REFLECT Identify creative companies.

You are going to read about creativity at work. Complete the chart with information about two creative companies you know about. Share your ideas with a group.

Company	How is it creative?
Apple	The phones and laptops look stylish. They make complicated software easy to use.

READ

WHAT DOES **CREATIVITY** AT **WORK MEAN?**

Traffic on streets like these in Bangkok, Thailand, might be improved by ride-sharing services like Grab.

A PREDICT Skim the article. What do you think it is mostly about?

a. How companies can help employees be more creative

b. How to get a job at a creative company

c. How creativity is important for businesses

1   How important is creativity at work? Very important. In a survey, top business people said that creativity is the most important factor for success. Often, we think that creativity is the ability to make beautiful things. For example, an artist is creative for making a painting. But in business, creativity often means **thinking of** new ideas that can **solve** difficult problems. And it's this kind of creativity that companies **value**.

2   One business that solves problems creatively is Grab. Grab is one of Asia's largest ride-hailing[1] companies. Malaysian-born Anthony Tan thought of Grab while talking to a friend. The friend **complained** that taxis in Malaysia were often unreliable[2] and expensive. Tan was interested in mobile technology. He knew about a company in California that was developing an app. The app let people get to places without taking taxis. In college, Tan developed an idea for his own ride-hailing app. He discussed the idea with his professors. They didn't think it would work. However, the idea won second place in a business competition. Soon after, Tan started Grab. After a few years, Grab was connecting people all over Asia. It made ride-hailing better and safer for riders and drivers.

3   But Grab wanted to find ways to be even more creative. Other ride-hailing companies, such as Uber, were taking away their customers. So, Grab spent $100 million on a new research lab. It **hired** software engineers and **data** analysts.

They **analyzed** data from the app. They wanted to find out what their users liked and needed. They tested new tools that offered food delivery, movie tickets, and financial services. Many of its 130 million users liked the new tools. "We've been bringing users to these businesses," Grab's co-founder says. "Now they can come to you."

4   In business, thinking of creative ideas isn't always easy. But there are several ways companies can be more creative. A creative business **aims** to:

▶ question the normal way of doing something and think of a new way;

▶ connect ideas from different fields and places;

▶ be open to making changes to improve sales;

▶ analyze data to get more information about customers;

▶ and **experiment** with ideas that might lead to new ways of thinking.

It's clear that creativity plays an important role in all companies. In today's fast-moving world, companies must be creative to succeed. And in order to be successful and to stay in business, companies need **employees** who are creative thinkers.

---

[1] **ride-hailing** (adj) using an app to get a car ride
[2] **unreliable** (adj) not to be trusted, particularly in terms of accuracy, honesty, or punctuality

B MAIN IDEAS What is the article mainly about? Choose the three main ideas.

a. Grab drivers are creative.

b. Companies use creativity to solve problems.

c. Grab offers a variety of services to its customers.

d. There are steps companies can take to be more creative.

e. Creative companies can improve their customers' lives.

CRITICAL THINKING   Question sources

As you read, ask yourself questions about the source of information. For example, paragraph 1 refers to a recent survey. Ask yourself when and where the survey was done. The date is especially important in evaluating how relevant the information is today.

READING SKILL Annotate a text

Annotating a text helps you stay focused as you read. It can also help you better identify and remember important information. Here are some ways to annotate a text:

- ▶ Highlight the main ideas. You can use different colors.
- ▶ Underline important details. Use different types of underlining (single line, double line, wavy line).
- ▶ Circle key words such as names, dates, and places.
- ▶ In the margin, note down the main idea of each paragraph. Use a few words, not a complete sentence.

C APPLY Annotate paragraphs 2 and 3 of the article. Compare your notes with a partner's.

D DETAILS Complete the chart. Use one word or number for each answer.

Behaviors of creative businesses	Grab's behaviors
Question the normal way of doing something, and think of a new way.	Anthony Tan wondered how taxis in 1_____ could be better. In college, he created a(n) 2_____ app. The app helped people get around without using 3_____.
Connect ideas from different fields and places.	Tan liked mobile 4_____ and heard about a company in 5_____ that was making a similar app.
Be open to making changes to improve sales.	Grab invested 6_____ in a new lab.
Analyze data to get more information about customers.	Grab looked at their data to see what their 7_____ wanted.
Experiment with ideas that might lead to new ways of thinking.	Grab experimented with new 8_____ that offered different services.

REFLECT   Evaluate creative behaviors.

Write answers to the questions in your notebook. Then discuss in a small group.

1. Think about the creative companies you identified earlier. Which behaviors from activity D do you think these companies have used?

2. Do you know anyone who is very creative? Give an example of how they are creative.

PREPARE TO READ

A VOCABULARY Complete the sentences with the correct form of the words. Use a dictionary if necessary.

actively (adv)	effective (adj)	otherwise (adv)	require (v)	trouble (n)
conscious (adj)	increase (v)	product (n)	separate (adj)	work on (v phr)

1. Many people buy household _____, like laundry detergent, from a supermarket.

2. The company needs to _____ their customer service. There have been several complaints recently.

3. Some people have _____ speaking in front of a large audience. They get very nervous.

4. When you are asleep, the _____ part of your brain isn't active.

5. Companies want to hire _____ employees who get their work done.

6. Companies must change when their customers' preferences change. _____, they might not stay in business.

7. Many jobs in the retail business _____ employees to work on weekends.

8. There is a lot of work to do in the coming months, so the company is _____ hiring new employees.

9. Many people like to keep their home life _____ from their work life.

10. According to some experts, listening to music _____ creativity because it helps you think of new ideas.

B PERSONALIZE Discuss these questions with a partner.

1. What is one area you can **work on** to improve your English?
2. What is an **effective** way that you handled a problem recently?
3. What are some tasks at work or at school that you have **trouble** with?

REFLECT Brainstorm ways to be more creative.

You are going to read about ways to be more creative. What are some ways you could be more creative at school or work? Write two ways. Then discuss your ideas with a partner.

_____

_____

_____

READ

A PREVIEW Answer the questions with a partner.

1. Read paragraph 1. What type of article is this?

   a. a science report

   b. an advice column

   c. a letter to the editor

2. How do you think this photo might relate to advice about being more creative?

TIPS FROM THE EXPERTS 🎧 7.2

Hi Experts!

1   I need help. My job **requires** me to think of ideas for new **products**. Sometimes I can't think of anything original. How can I be more creative?

Thanks!

Dear Reader,

2   I'm glad you asked! Creativity at work is really important. Improving your ability to think outside the box[1] can help you become a more **effective** employee. So, how can you think more creatively? Here are some tips!

3   First, walk more. According to a recent study, walking can **increase** your creativity. Researchers used a test to measure creativity. The test asks people to think of new uses for a common object, such as a shoe. Some people thought of ideas while sitting and others while walking. Then the researchers counted the useful and original ideas that people wrote down. The walkers had more of these ideas than the sitters did. However, it can't be just any kind of walking. Walking fast with a fixed[2] plan for your walk doesn't have a positive effect on creativity. Only walking at a comfortable speed without a fixed plan increases a person's creative thinking skills.

4   Next, try drawing. Research has shown that drawing can help you think about things differently. It does this by using parts of the brain that are not used when a person is just listening or thinking. You don't have to be a professional artist to benefit from drawing.

Just doodling[3] pictures as you consider a problem can help you think of ideas you wouldn't be able to think of **otherwise**. One expert suggests some ways to let doodling make you more creative. For example, you can think of two different things, like a house and a cat, and draw their **separate** parts. Then combine those parts to create new things, like a door with eyes or a window with feet. This can help you think of unusual ideas.

5   One final tip is to forget about the problem you are trying to solve. Yes, to solve a problem, it might actually help to stop thinking about it and do something else. A researcher discovered that when people stop **actively** thinking about a problem, their minds continue to **work on** finding an answer. This happens even while they are doing something else. According to another expert, this is because the subconscious mind is so much better at problem solving than the **conscious** mind is. So the next time you are having **trouble** thinking of a good idea, chat with a colleague or clean your desk for a while before thinking about it more.

Good luck!

---

[1]**think outside the box** (v phr) to think in a creative and unusual way

[2]**fixed** (adj) set; not changing

[3]**doodle** (v) to draw pictures or patterns while you think of other things

People walk along a foot bridge in Plitvice Lakes National Park, a UNESCO World Heritage site in Croatia.

Doodling at work

B Read paragraphs 4 and 5 again. Annotate them as you read.

C **MAIN IDEAS** What tips do the experts give? Complete the main ideas with one word from the article.

If you want to think more creatively:

1. Go for a _____.

2. _____ a picture to think about things differently.

3. _____ thinking about the problem.

D **DETAILS** Choose the correct answer to complete each sentence.

1. Researchers asked participants to think of **uses for / types of** common objects.
2. Participants who were **sitting / walking** thought of more ideas.
3. Walking **quickly / slowly** helped participants become more creative.
4. Walking **with / without** a fixed route increased people's creativity.
5. Drawing helps you be more creative by turning **on / off** unused parts of the brain.
6. To increase your creativity, try drawing combinations of two **similar / different** things.
7. You should **keep thinking about it / think about something else** when you have difficulty solving a problem.
8. The **conscious / subconscious** brain is better at solving problems.

REFLECT Apply tips to be creative.

Choose one of the common student problems below. Which of the strategies from the article could help solve it? Write your ideas in your notebook. Then discuss with a partner.

▶ deciding which classes to take

▶ remembering where you left a lost item

▶ choosing a topic for an essay

▶ trying to understand a difficult idea in class

▶ preparing for a test or exam

WRITE

You are going to write an essay for a job or college application which asks: "Identify a problem and explain how to solve it creatively." Use the ideas, vocabulary, and skills from the unit.

A MODEL Read the essay. Underline the topic sentences of the two body paragraphs.

Creative Ways to Make Extra Money

If you have a full-time job, you expect to make enough money to live comfortably. Unfortunately, salaries are not rising for many employees. This makes it hard for some people to pay for even the basic things like food and housing. What can you do? How can you earn extra money if you already have a full-time job? I propose two creative ways to earn extra money when your full-time job does not pay enough.

One way to earn more money is to do small "side" or part-time jobs. For example, you might take part in a focus group. A focus group is when a company asks possible customers to give feedback on a product. Some companies pay up to $200 for a couple of hours of work. Another good side job is working for a caterer. Caterers prepare and serve food at parties and events. They frequently need part-time help at these events. If you enjoy meeting new people, catering might be a fun way to make $15 to $20 an hour on the weekend.

Another way to earn extra money is to sell items online. First of all, you could start selling clothes that you don't wear anymore. Choose a used clothing app and set up an account. It's surprising how many people buy used clothes online. Another possibility, if you enjoy working with your hands, is selling used furniture. In many cities, people leave unwanted furniture on the street. You could repair and paint the furniture and then sell your products online.

If you already have a full-time job, but you still have money problems, you may need to come up with a creative solution. Two possibilities are working at a part-time or side job and selling items online.

B ANALYZE THE MODEL Answer the questions about the model essay.

Body paragraph 1

Topic sentence: One way to earn more money is to do small "side" or part-time jobs.

Supporting ideas: _____

_____

Body paragraph 2

Topic sentence: Another way to earn extra money is to sell items online.

Supporting ideas: _____

_____

WRITING SKILL Write an introductory paragraph

The **introductory paragraph** gives the reader background information and states the main idea of the essay. The paragraph often begins with a **hook**. A hook can be a surprising fact or a question. It gets the reader interested in the topic.

Over 75 percent of employers said that creativity is the most important quality they look for in an employee. (fact)

Research suggests employers value creativity. But is creativity really that useful at work? (question)

The **thesis statement** states the main idea of the essay. It includes the topic and the writer's specific or **controlling idea** about the topic. It usually appears at the end of the introductory paragraph.

<u>*To solve the problem of boredom at work*</u>, <u>*I suggest two solutions*</u>.
          topic   controlling idea

C APPLY Look again at the model essay. Complete the tasks.

1. Underline the hook. Which type of hook did the writer use?

    a. provided a fact   b. asked a question

2. Underline the thesis statement. What are the topic and the writer's specific idea?

    Topic: _____

    Writer's specific idea: _____

3. Write an alternative thesis statement for the model essay.

    _____.

GRAMMAR Verbs followed by gerunds or infinitives

Some verbs can be followed by a gerund.

avoid   discuss   enjoy   finish   include   keep   practice   suggest

> My friend **suggested looking** for a second job.
>
> I **avoided working** when I was a student.

Some verbs can be followed by an infinitive.

agree   ask   choose   decide   hope   learn   need   plan   want

> I **needed to make** more money if I **wanted to go** on the trip.
>
> The company **plans to grow** in the next five years.

Some verbs can be followed by either a gerund or an infinitive. The meaning is usually the same.

begin   continue   hate   like   love   prefer   start   try

> My savings **started to grow** immediately.
>
> My savings **started growing** immediately.

D GRAMMAR Find and underline examples of verbs + gerunds and verbs + infinitives in the body paragraphs of the model essay.

E GRAMMAR Choose the gerund or infinitive to complete the sentence. If both are possible, choose both.

1. The company decided **creating / to create** more quiet spaces for their employees.

2. Some people prefer **working / to work** on projects in a group.

3. Experts suggest **practicing / to practice** creativity to develop problem-solving skills.

4. To stay creative, some people need **changing / to change** jobs every few years.

5. If I avoid **thinking / to think** about a problem, the solution often comes to me.

6. The group began **discussing / to discuss** creative ways to save money.

7. When you brainstorm, keep **writing / to write** ideas even if they don't seem useful.

8. I like **researching / to research** ideas for saving money.

9. Her boss agreed **to let / letting** her go on vacation next month.

10. Our task includes **to find / finding** solutions to common problems.

11. Employers hope **to hire / hiring** workers who know how to solve problems.

12. Practice to **write / writing** a hook in your introductory paragraph.

F GRAMMAR Complete the sentences with your own ideas. Use gerunds or infinitives.

1. When I am studying, I like _____.

2. My friend needed _____, so I offered to help.

3. When I have trouble with a subject in school, I try _____.

4. I try to avoid _____.

5. Being a student involves _____.

G EDIT Read the introductory and body paragraph. Find and correct five errors with gerunds and infinitives.

Creative Ways to Remember New Information

Is it possible to improve your memory (and improve your grades)? Having a good memory is important for success in school. I have a poor memory. I decided learning about history, but I can't remember all of the details. I study hard, but I keep to forget important information. However, there are ways to improve your memory. Most people will enjoy to try them out. Sleeping after studying and playing games are two creative ways to improve your memory.

One way to improve your memory is sleeping. Experts suggest to go to bed right after you study because you remember new information better. Let's say you learn something new and then do something else, like watch TV. Your brain wants processing the information in the TV show. As a result, the information you studied is less likely to get into your long-term memory.

A man lying down for a nap among orphaned baby rhinos in Lewa Wildlife Conservancy, Kenya

PLAN & WRITE

H BRAINSTORM In the chart, write three problems that are common at school or work (e.g., bad grades, low pay). Then brainstorm and write two creative ways to solve each problem.

Problem	Possible solutions
	1.
	2.
	1.
	2.
	1.
	2.

I OUTLINE Choose the problem from activity H with the most creative solutions. Complete the outline for your essay.

Title: _____

Introductory paragraph

Hook: _____

Thesis statement: _____

First body paragraph

Solution 1 Topic sentence: _____

Supporting idea 1: _____

Supporting idea 2: _____

Second body paragraph (2nd solution)

Solution 2 Topic sentence: _____

Supporting idea 1: _____

Supporting idea 2: _____

Concluding paragraph

Suggested solution: _____

One way to organize a problem-solution essay is to first explain the problem in the introductory paragraph. Then use each body paragraph to explain a different solution. You can end the essay by suggesting which solution you think is the best one.

J FIRST DRAFT Use your outline to write a first draft of your essay.

K REVISE Use this list as you write your second draft.

- ☐ Does your thesis statement state the main idea of your entire essay?
- ☐ Does your introductory paragraph give background on the topic?
- ☐ Does your introductory paragraph include a hook? What type is it?
- ☐ Is there any information that doesn't belong?

L EDIT Use this list as you write your final draft.

- ☐ Did you use infinitives and gerunds correctly?
- ☐ Do your subjects and verbs agree?
- ☐ Did you spell all the words correctly?
- ☐ Did you use correct punctuation?

M FINAL DRAFT Reread your essay and correct any errors. Then submit it to your teacher.

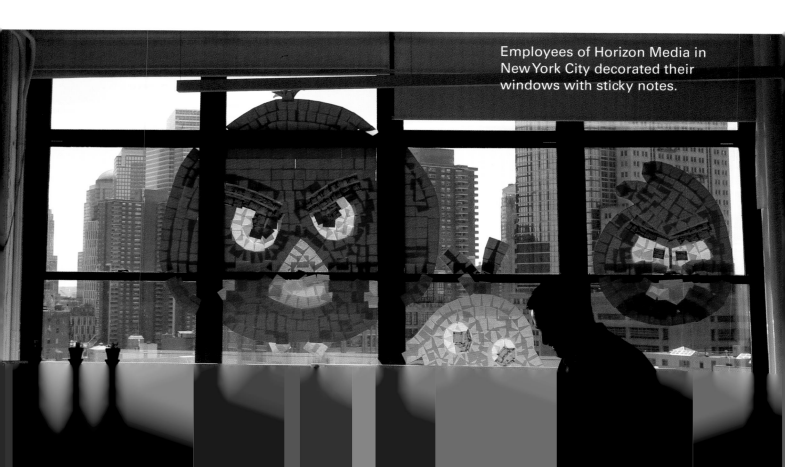

Employees of Horizon Media in New York City decorated their windows with sticky notes.

REFLECT

A Check (✓) the Reflect activities you can do and the academic skills you can use.

- ☐ identify creative companies
- ☐ evaluate creative behaviors
- ☐ brainstorm ways to be more creative
- ☐ apply tips to be creative
- ☐ write an essay about how to solve a problem creatively

- ☐ annotate a text
- ☐ write an introductory paragraph
- ☐ verbs followed by gerunds or infinitives
- ☐ question sources

B Write the vocabulary words from the unit in the correct column. Add any other words that you learned. Circle words you still need to practice.

NOUN	VERB	ADJECTIVE	ADVERB & OTHER

C Reflect on the ideas in the unit as you answer these questions.

1. What information about creativity in this unit was new to you?

_____

_____

_____

2. Will any of the ideas in this unit help you be more creative at work or at school? Explain.

_____

_____

_____

LOW-TECH LEARNING

Girls performing an experiment in a science class in Al-Maarifa Girls Secondary School, Bahrain

CONNECT TO THE TOPIC

1. How are the students in the photo learning?

2. What are some effective ways to learn something new?

National Geographic Explorer Maritza Morales Casanova trains children to care for the environment in Tesoco Nuevo, Yucatán, Mexico.

THEME-PARK **CLASSROOM**

A Watch the video about Ms. Morales's classroom. Then choose the correct words to complete the statements. ▶ 8.1

1. Morales says her job is to teach children to **pass tests / teach others**.
2. She wants them to learn how to **grow food / protect Earth**.
3. Her classroom is **indoors / outdoors**.
4. Her students learn about trees by **watching videos / planting seeds**.
5. The classroom **has / doesn't have** chairs and tables.
6. She uses **her own / computer** games in the classroom.

B Watch the video again. Then write your answers to the questions. Discuss your ideas with a partner. ▶ 8.1

1. Why do you think Morales loves her job? _____

2. Why do you think children might like being in her classroom?

_____

BEFORE YOU READ

A VOCABULARY Write the words next to their definitions. Use a dictionary if necessary.

access (n)	development (n)	intelligence (n)	obvious (adj)	physical (adj)
acquire (v)	former (adj)	invent (v)	performance (n)	preferable (adj)

1. _____: growth

2. _____: the ability to do something

3. _____: relating to the body

4. _____: better, more suitable

5. _____: the ability or right to use something

6. _____: clear and easy to see or understand

7. _____: to get; to learn

8. _____: create something new (usually a product)

9. _____: the ability to learn about and understand things

10. _____: past; earlier

B PERSONALIZE Discuss these questions with a partner.

1. What are some **obvious** differences between elementary and high schools?
2. What kinds of **physical** activities did you do in elementary school?
3. How could you improve your **performance** on school tests?

REFLECT Assess technology for young learners.

You are going to read about low-tech schools. Discuss these questions in a small group.

1. Which of the following technologies do you think is the most helpful for young learners? Choose the best one or add your own idea.

   laptops   tablets   e-books   Internet

   _____

2. Do you think it's important for young learners to use technology? Explain.

   _____

   _____

READ

LOW-TECH,
HIGH-PLAY SCHOOLS

A PREVIEW Read the title and look at the photo. What do you think children do in a low-tech, high-play classroom? Discuss your answers in a small group.

B MAIN IDEAS Read the article. Then complete the summary with the correct form of the words.

development	grade	harmful	low-tech	skill

Some parents think that ed tech is [1]_____ for children. Studies show that ed tech can lower [2]_____ and affect children's physical [3]_____. Other studies suggest that a focus on ed tech is not teaching children the [4]_____ they need in the future. Because of this, some parents are sending their children to [5]_____ schools.

These children learn about planting.

1   Since the mid-2000s, schools have spent billions of dollars on ed tech[1]. Ed tech includes computers, tablets, and laptops used for learning. The benefits seem **obvious**. Students like ed tech because it's fun. Many teachers like it because it adds variety to the classroom. Administrators[2] think that ed tech prepares children for college and work. Although ed tech has a lot to offer students, some parents think that a low-tech learning environment might be **preferable.**

2   Too much ed tech in the classroom may be harmful to young learners. Some studies suggest that ed tech affects student **performance**. A recent study found that the more time students spent looking at a screen, the lower their grades were. Additional research shows that too much screen time can harm children's **physical development**. Most people believe that children should be playing games and being active. Finally, according to the OECD[3], ed tech is not helping students **acquire** "new skills." These skills are the ones children need for future jobs. They include creativity, emotional **intelligence**, and self-determination[4].

3   In response to this research, some parents are sending their children to low-tech schools. A low-tech school limits **access** to ed tech in the classroom. Instead, students use a lot of experiential learning. In other words, they learn by doing. One example is Brightworks School in San Francisco. It was founded by Gever Tulley, a **former** software engineer. Like traditional schools, Brightworks wants to prepare students for the future. Tulley, however, thinks that traditional schools aren't working for a lot of children.

4   At Brightworks, students do projects that they **invent** themselves. They do many of these projects in groups. For example, children at the lower levels learn math by building large structures with their classmates. Unlike traditional schools, there are few desks and chairs. And there are no screens. Instead, teachers help students to discover their own abilities—often in treehouse classrooms. Importantly, there are no tests or grading. The focus is on enjoying the process of learning, not on the results. "I like to think of our school as a huge lab for learning and play," says Tulley.

5   Interestingly, over 60 percent of the students at Brightworks are from tech families. Parents of these students work in California's large tech industry. Other low-tech schools in the area are popular with tech families, too. For many people, there is no area of life that is free from smartphones, tablets, and laptops. But maybe there should be a tech-free area of life, at least for children.

---

[1]**ed tech** (n phr) an abbreviation of educational technology

[2]**administrators** (n) people who manage or supervise

[3]**OECD** Organization for Economic Co-operation and Development

[4]**self-determination** (n) the ability to decide what you are going to do without being told by someone else

READING SKILL   Distinguish between facts and opinions

It is important to be able to identify whether what you read is a fact or an opinion. A fact is something that is true and can be proven. An opinion is what someone thinks.

Fact: *Ed tech includes computers, tablets, and laptops used for learning purposes.*

Opinion: *School administrators believe access to ed tech helps prepare children for the future.*

The following words and phrases signal that something is an opinion:

Some people think…   *It is believed…*   *possibly*   *might*   *maybe*

C APPLY Read the statements from the article. Write F for *Fact* or O for *Opinion*.

1. _____ Administrators believe ed tech prepares children for college and work.

2. _____ A recent study found that the more time students spent looking at a screen, the lower their grades were.

3. _____ In response to this research, some parents are sending their children to low-tech schools.

4. _____ One example is Brightworks School in San Francisco.

5. _____ Interestingly, over 60 percent of the students at Brightworks are from tech families.

6. _____ But maybe there should be a tech-free area of life, at least for children.

D DETAILS Write the different practices of each school (a–f) in the correct place in the Venn diagram.

a. Spends a lot of money on ed tech

b. Thinks they are preparing students for the future

c. Lets students create their own projects

d. Limits the amount of ed tech

e. Isn't very focused on tests and grades

f. Expects students to sit at desks

g. Has students use ed tech to learn

h. Often has classes outside

Traditional schools

Brightworks

REFLECT   Relate ideas to your education.

Discuss your answers in a small group.

1. When you were a child, was your school a high-tech school or a low-tech school?

2. What is your most recent experience with technology at school?

PREPARE TO READ

A VOCABULARY
Complete the sentences with the correct form of the words. Use a dictionary if necessary.

argue (v)	convenient (adj)	look up (v phr)	nearby (adj)	strategy (n)
combination (n)	distracting (adj)	material (n)	relevant (adj)	tend to (v phr)

1. Smartphones can be _____, which makes them dangerous when driving.

2. Types of reading _____ in college include textbooks, novels, and articles.

3. People _____ check their phones for messages as soon as they get a notification.

4. Technology makes life easier in a lot of ways. However, some people _____ that we rely on it too much.

5. Learning should be _____ to students and give them what they need.

6. Annotating a text is one _____ that you can use to improve your reading.

7. A smartphone is a _____ of a computer, a camera, and a phone.

8. It's easy to _____ the definition of a word in a dictionary.

9. Delivery apps make getting food very _____. Instead of going out to a store, you can order anything online and have it delivered to your house.

10. People depend on their phones so much that they always have them _____.

B PERSONALIZE
Discuss these questions with a partner.

1. What kinds of information do you **look up** on your phone?
2. When do you **tend to** do your homework?
3. What are some **strategies** you use to remember new vocabulary?

REFLECT Consider technology for learning new information.

You are going to read about using technology in college. Discuss the questions in a small group.

1. How do you use technology to learn new information? Complete the chart with your ideas.

Technology in the classroom	Technology outside the classroom

2. What are the most useful technologies for learning English?

READ

LAPTOPS AT COLLEGE: PROS AND CONS

The library at National Autonomous University of Mexico (UNAM) in Mexico City, Mexico

A PREDICT What do you think the pros and cons of using laptops in college might be? Discuss your ideas with a partner.

1   Many students use a laptop in college. In fact, a recent survey found that 81% of college students depend on their laptop. While a laptop can be useful in college, some **argue** that it might actually make learning less effective. Here are pros and cons of using a laptop to read e-books and take notes in college.

Reading e-books on a laptop

2   The advantages of e-books are clear. They may be cheaper than traditional print books. Accessing a lot of e-books on a laptop is also **convenient**. It's easy to highlight important information and quickly **look up** words online. Finally, e-books take up a lot less space and are much easier to carry around.

3   However, some research suggests that we don't read as deeply when we read e-books. In fact, people who read e-books **tend to** skim. Studies that track eye movement show that readers tend to move their eyes around the page when they read screens. On the other hand, people read more linearly[1] when they read a print book. Some people think e-books are **distracting**, too. This is because it's easy to stop reading and open another app or click on a word or phrase you want to look up. Because of this, some studies show that readers of e-books remember less of what they read than readers of print books.

Taking lecture notes with a laptop

4   Typing lecture notes is faster on a laptop than writing them by hand. You can look up **relevant** information as you type. Because they're typed, notes are easier to read later when it's time to review. Typed notes are easier to organize or reorganize, too.

You can make outlines and bulleted or numbered lists with the click of a button.

5   Not using a laptop to take lecture notes has its advantages too. A recent study showed that writing notes by hand helps students perform better. When you write notes by hand you understand and remember information that you heard in a lecture. Why? Taking notes by hand is slower. It gives you the opportunity to process the information you're taking notes on. When you type on a laptop, you aren't actually thinking about what you're writing. Instead, you are just transcribing—writing what you hear word-for-word.

Top tech learning tips

To get the best out of your laptop in college, try a **combination** of the following low- and high-tech **strategies**.

- ▶ Take lecture notes by hand. Then use your notes to create a digital document later.

- ▶ Have a notebook **nearby** to write down main ideas and details from an e-book.

- ▶ Write down questions you have about the **material** in your notebook. Look up the answers after you've finished reading.

- ▶ If you see words you don't know while reading an e-book, write them down and look them up later.

[1]**linearly** (adv) (when reading) from left to right across the text

---

B MAIN IDEAS Write the correct paragraph number (2-5) next to its main idea. One idea is extra.

a. _____ There are few advantages to using technology in college.

b. _____ Taking notes by hand has some benefits over typing notes.

c. _____ There are advantages to using e-books instead of traditional books.

d. _____ There are several advantages to typing your notes.

e. _____ Using e-books is not always the most effective way to read.

The Chinese University
of Hong Kong Library

C DETAILS Read the sentences. Write T for *True*, F for *False*, or NG for *Not Given*.

1. _____ It is easier to buy e-books than traditional books.

2. _____ We read better when we read e-books.

3. _____ We take notes more quickly when we type them.

4. _____ We remember more when we write notes by hand than when we type them.

5. _____ If you have questions about your reading material or new words, you should look up the answers while you read.

6. _____ You should write your lecture notes by hand and type them up later.

D Read the statements from the article. Write F for *Fact* or O for *Opinion*.

1. _____ A recent survey found that 81% of college students depend on a laptop.

2. _____ People who read e-books tend to skim.

3. _____ Some people think e-books are distracting, too.

4. _____ A recent study showed that writing notes by hand helps students perform better.

REFLECT   Evaluate tech learning tips.

Which of the "Top Tech Learning Tips" do you think are the most useful? Which will you try?
Write your answers in a notebook. Then discuss them with a partner.

WRITE

UNIT TASK Write an essay about ed tech.

You are going to write an essay in response to the question: "Which is better, low-tech or high-tech learning?" Use the ideas, skills, and vocabulary from this unit.

A MODEL ESSAY Read the essay for the question: "Is going to college worth the time and money?" Underline the thesis statement.

Should You Go To College?

Is going to college really worth the cost? Some people think that going to college costs too much money and time. Other people argue that you don't need a college degree to find a good job. As a result, many people wonder if a college education is a waste of time and money. In my view, getting a college degree is a path to financial success and overall happiness.

First of all, a college degree has financial benefits. College graduates are more likely to find work since most professional jobs require a college degree. Also, salaries for college grads are usually higher than for high school graduates. College graduates are in a better financial situation than non-graduates even though many have large loans to pay off.

Second, college graduates enjoy their jobs more. They are much more likely to find a job they like than people without a college education. College allows a student to get the necessary degree for a wide variety of professions. For example, a student can become an engineer, nurse, or computer programmer. Although it is possible to work hard and be successful without a college degree, you have more options with a college degree. This means college grads are more likely to be interested in their work and, therefore, happier.

While a college education can be expensive, it's clear that it is not a waste of money or time. Getting a degree can lead to financial success and happiness. Anyone who has the opportunity to attend college should definitely go.

CRITICAL THINKING   Evaluate the practicality of advice

When you read a writer's advice in an article, decide whether it is practical or useful. Don't just accept the advice without evaluating it first. It may not make sense for your situation.

B ANALYZE THE MODEL Complete the outline of the model essay.

Title: _____

Introductory Paragraph

Hook: _____

Thesis statement: _____

_____.

First Body Paragraph

Reason 1: A college degree has _____.

Supporting idea 1: _____

Supporting idea 2: _____

Second Body Paragraph

Reason 2: College graduates _____.

Supporting idea 1: _____

Supporting idea 2: _____

Concluding Paragraph

It's clear that a college education is not a _____.

WRITING SKILL **Write a concluding paragraph**

The **concluding paragraph** of an essay usually begins with a summary statement and ends with a final thought.

The **summary statement** restates the thesis statement from the introductory paragraph. It reminds the reader of the main idea of the essay, but uses different words.

Thesis statement: *In my view, all students should study a foreign language.*

Summary statement: *While some students might not see the importance of a second language, learning a second language has many real benefits.*

Here are three ways to write a **final thought**.

▶ Opinion: *With a second language, you are better prepared for the 21ˢᵗ century.*

▶ Prediction: *People who can speak a second language might have more job opportunities.*

▶ Question: *Will more people begin to realize the benefits of learning a second language?*

C APPLY Look at the model essay again and complete the tasks.

1. Reread the concluding paragraph. Underline the summary statement.

2. What type of final thought did the writer use in the model essay?

   a. prediction   b. question   c. opinion

3. Write an alternate final thought.

   _____

   _____

GRAMMAR   Adverb clauses of contrast

An **adverb clause of contrast** introduces an idea that is different from the idea in the main clause. Adverb clauses of contrast start with a connecting word like: *while, although,* or *even though,* and are followed by a subject + verb.

> **<u>While</u> some believe college is a waste of money,** *I think it's worth the money.*

> **<u>Although</u> I took many college classes,** *I never graduated from college.*

> *I never graduated from college* **<u>even though</u> I attended classes for years**.

Note that when the adverb clause comes first in a sentence, a comma separates it from the main clause.

D GRAMMAR Find and underline the three adverb clauses of contrast in the model essay. Draw two lines under each connecting word.

E GRAMMAR Combine the sentences using adverb clauses of contrast. More than one answer is possible.

1. Speaking another language prepares you for different jobs.
   Learning a second language may be difficult.

   _____

   _____

2. Experiential learning lets children develop life-long skills.
   Classrooms in low-tech schools might seem disorganized.

   _____

   _____

3. Many college graduates will have trouble paying off large loans.
   College graduates may find higher-paying jobs.

   _____

   _____

A student of Handan No.1 High School in Handan, China, studies for the upcoming national college entrance examination.

F GRAMMAR Write statements with adverb clauses of contrast about the following topics.

1. taking classes that you're not interested in

   _____

   _____

2. attending a high-tech elementary school

   _____

   _____

3. using a laptop in class

   _____

   _____

4. attending an expensive, private university

   _____

   _____

5. taking out a student loan

   _____

   _____

G EDIT Read the body paragraphs from an opinion essay about education. Find and correct three errors with adverb clauses of contrast.

Do Grades Matter?

Most of us are used to receiving grades at school. Traditionally, colleges have used a five-point grading system to evaluate students. While this system is familiar some colleges have started moving to a no-grade system. In my opinion, a system that does not use grades is the right approach to evaluating a student's performance.

No-grade schools have a much less competitive atmosphere. Even some competition is good for us, it can cause stress and anxiety for many students. In fact, a recent study showed that worrying about grades led students to get psychological help. Another study showed that students who attend non-grading schools have better mental health in general. Although many students in traditional colleges may seem happy. Students at no-grade schools visit counseling services less often.

PLAN & WRITE

H BRAINSTORM Think about the question you are going to write about: "Which is better, low-tech or high-tech learning?" Consider the topics below. Then complete the chart with reasons on both sides of the issue.

Student grades

Students' physical and emotional well-being

Skills taught/learned

Cost of schools

Teacher/administrator roles

Parent expectations

Reasons for low-tech learning	Reasons for high-tech learning

WRITING TIP

When you write an opinion essay, you should include opposing ideas or opinions and say why they are not as strong as your own opinion. Adverb clauses of contrast are often used in this situation.

While learning a language might be time-consuming and expensive, it can change your life for the better.

I OUTLINE Complete the outline with your ideas. Use the ideas from your brainstorming.

Title: _____

Introductory paragraph

Hook: _____

Thesis statement (Opinion): _____

_____

First body paragraph

Reason 1: _____

Supporting idea: _____

Supporting idea: _____

Second body paragraph

Reason 2: _____

Supporting idea: _____

Supporting idea: _____

Concluding paragraph

Summary statement: _____

Final thought: _____

J FIRST DRAFT Use your outline to write a first draft of your essay.

K REVISE Use this list as you write your second draft.

- ☐ Does your thesis statement state your opinion?
- ☐ Does your introductory paragraph include a hook?
- ☐ Does each body paragraph include a reason that supports your opinion?
- ☐ Does your concluding paragraph have a summary statement and a final thought?
- ☐ Is there any information that doesn't belong?

L EDIT Use this list as you write your final draft.

- ☐ Did you use adverb clauses of contrast correctly?
- ☐ Do your subjects and verbs agree?
- ☐ Did you spell all the words correctly?
- ☐ Did you use correct punctuation?

M FINAL DRAFT Reread your essay and correct any errors. Then submit it to your teacher.

REFLECT

A Check (✓) the Reflect activities you can do and the academic skills you can use.

- ☐ assess technology for young learners
- ☐ relate ideas to your education
- ☐ consider technology for learning new information
- ☐ evaluate tech learning tips
- ☐ write an essay about ed tech

- ☐ distinguish between facts and opinions
- ☐ write a concluding paragraph
- ☐ adverb clauses of contrast
- ☐ evaluate the practicality of advice

B Write the vocabulary words from the unit in the correct column. Add any other words that you learned. Circle words you still need to practice.

NOUN	VERB	ADJECTIVE	ADVERB & OTHER

C Reflect on the ideas in the unit as you answer these questions.

1. What is one example of how you use technology effectively at school or in college?

_____

_____

_____

2. What ideas or skills in this unit will be most useful to you in the future?

_____

_____

_____

Polysemy Multiple-meaning words

Polysemy refers to a word that has two or more different meanings. Sometimes the meanings are similar but are not exactly the same.

For example, *head* can mean "a leader" or "the body part on top of your neck." Sometimes one word can be different parts of speech. The word *head* can also be a verb meaning "to lead." Use context clues—the words before and after a word—to help you decide which meaning is correct.

A Choose the best meaning of the words in bold. Use context clues to help. Check your answers in a dictionary.

1. The student **gathered** information for the project.

   a. people came together   b. collected things or ideas

2. Tourists and residents love to relax in the **public** gardens in London.

   a. open to everyone   b. all people

3. The **design** for the new school was very modern.

   a. a decoration   b. a plan

4. Many leaders think safety is the main **issue** for their communities.

   a. a problem   b. the most recent edition of a newspaper or magazine

5. One **sign** of stress is weight loss.

   a. information on display   b. an indication something is happening

Connotation

Connotation means the positive, negative, or neutral feeling of a word.

For example, *home, house,* and *shelter* all mean places that people live. But *home* usually connotes a positive feeling of warmth and safety. The word *house* has a more neutral feeling, while *shelter* connotes a temporary or very basic place to live.

B Complete the chart with the words in the box. Use a thesaurus or dictionary to help you.

achieve	bargain	cheap	expert
odd	recommend	suggest	unique

Positive	Neutral	Negative
genius		know-it-all
	low-cost	
	unusual	
	deal with (something)	get (something) over with
		warn

Prefix *mis-*

Prefixes come at the beginning of words. They change the meaning of a word. The prefix *mis-* means "bad" or "wrong." You can add *mis-* to some words to change their meanings.

mis- + *lead* = **mis**lead, meaning "to lead someone to think that something is not true"

A Choose the correct word to complete each sentence. Check your answers in a dictionary.

1. Some social media sites contain **misleading / misunderstanding** information.

2. It is easy to **miscalculate / misunderstand** someone when they don't speak your language well.

3. A company can go out of business if it is **misused / mismanaged**.

4. People from different cultures sometimes **misunderstand / mismanage** each other.

5. I thought I could catch the train in time, but I **misled / miscalculated**. It takes 15 minutes, not 10, to get to the station.

Using a dictionary Synonyms

Synonyms are words that are similar in meaning. The words *large* and *big* are synonyms. A dictionary may include synonyms for common words. These words may be set in a box labeled *Thesaurus* or marked *SYN*. You can also look for synonyms in a thesaurus.

THESAURUS

small (adj) little, tiny, minor

B Use a dictionary. Find the best synonym for the meanings of the words in bold.

1. **silent** (adj) not talking

   a. still   b. mute

2. **avoid** (v) to not do something

   a. refrain   b. bypass

3. **unkind** (adj) mean

   a. unfeeling   b. cruel

4. **rule** (n) a general condition

   a. line   b. method

5. **recognize** (v) to remember someone when you hear or see them

   a. identify   b. acknowledge

Suffix -ment

Suffixes come at the end of words. They change the form of a word. The suffix -ment often means "an action or result of an action." You can add -ment to some verbs to make nouns.

VERB + -MENT = NOUN

achieve + **ment** = *achieve***ment** (When you achieve something, it's an achievement.)

move + **ment** = *move***ment** (When something moves, you see movement.)

A Complete each sentence with a noun. Use the verbs in the box and -*ment*. One word is extra.

advertise	enjoy	entertain	equip	improve	move

1. The _____ industry produces a lot of scary movies and TV shows.

2. Companies use _____ to sell their products. You see them on TV.

3. You need special _____, like headsets, to use virtual reality (VR).

4. My new computer is an _____ over my old one. It is much faster.

5. I don't get _____ from cooking. I prefer going out to eat.

Base words and affixes

A base word is a word that can't be broken into smaller words. For example, *happy* is a base word. You can sometimes add affixes—suffixes or prefixes—to a base word.

happy + **ness** = *happi***ness**   **un** + *happy* = **un***happy*

A dictionary will often list common affixes that you can add to a base word.

B Add the correct affix to each base word. More than one answer may be possible. Use a dictionary to help you.

Prefix	Suffix	
mis-	-ence	-ment
un-	-er	-y

1. _____ inspiring

2. achieve _____

3. challenge _____

4. risk _____

5. _____ use

6. prefer _____

Prefixes *in-*, *im-*, and *un-*

Prefixes come at the beginning of words. They change the meaning of a word. You can add the prefixes *in-*, *im-*, and *un-* to some adjectives and verbs to give them the opposite meaning.

> *in* + *expensive* = *inexpensive*, meaning "not expensive"

Look in a dictionary to check for the correct spelling.

A Add *im-*, *in-*, or *un-* to the words to make a word opposite in meaning. Use a dictionary if necessary.

1. ability: _____

2. familiar: _____

3. original: _____

4. possible: _____

5. professional: _____

6. polite: _____

Suffix *-al*

The suffix *-al* means "relating to." It is often used at the end of an adjective. For example, *global* means "relating to the whole world or globe."

When you see a new adjective ending with *-al*, you have a clue to help you understand the meaning of the word.

B Complete each sentence using an adjective from the box.

industrial	international	normal	professional	virtual

1. Today, many businesses think it is _____ for employees to work from a home.

2. Robots were first used in _____ settings like factories.

3. Many employees have _____ meetings—they meet online from their homes.

4. English has become a(n) _____ language—there are English speakers in most countries around the world today.

5. You look more _____ wearing business clothes to a job interview.

Compound words

A closed compound word is formed when two words are joined together to make a new word. A closed compound word may sometimes be joined with a hyphen (-).

    lifetime   part-time   airplane

Open compound words are not joined together but are still considered compound words.

    living room   high school

A   Match the parts of the compound words. Write the new word. Use a dictionary to help with spelling.

1.	back	a.	sense	_____
2.	sight	b.	ground	_____
3.	common	c.	card	_____
4.	credit	d.	where	_____
5.	every	e.	seeing	_____
6.	fast	f.	scape	_____
7.	land	g.	lasting	_____
8.	long-	h.	food	_____

Suffix -en

The suffix *-en* means "to cause to be or have." You can add *-en* to some nouns and adjectives to make verbs.

NOUN/ADJECTIVE + *-EN* = VERB

threat + **en** = *threat***en**, meaning "to cause threats"
weak + **en** = *weak***en**, meaning "to cause something to become weak"

B   Choose the correct form of the words to complete the paragraph.

Hurricanes [1]**threat / threaten** many parts of the world, particularly the United States and Japan. Hurricanes [2]**strength / strengthen** over warm ocean waters before hitting land. During a hurricane, the sky gets [3]**dark / darken**, the wind howls, and heavy rain falls. Water at the shore can rise to a [4]**height / heighten** of several meters, causing flooding. After they make landfall, hurricanes usually [5]**weak / weaken**.

Degrees of meaning

Antonyms are words that are opposite in meaning. The words *ugly* and *beautiful* are antonyms. However, between antonyms, there are other words that can have a range of meanings—for example, from "most positive" to "least positive."

MOST POSITIVE   LEAST POSITIVE

⟵──⟶

beautiful   attractive   plain   ugly

A Complete the lists that show different degrees of meaning. Use the words in the box.

huge	loud	never	often
silent	small	unique	wrong

⟵──⟶

1. perfect   accurate   imperfect   _____

2. frequently   _____   sometimes   _____

3. common   different   rare   _____

4. _____   quiet   noisy   _____

5. tiny   _____   large   _____

Suffix -*ly*

You can add the suffix -*ly* to some adjectives to form adverbs. The suffix -*ly* means "in a particular way." For adjectives ending in -*le*, remove the -*e* and add -*y*. For adjectives ending in -*y*, change the -*y* to an -*i*.

ADJECTIVE + -*LY* = ADVERB
beautiful + -**ly** = *beautiful**ly***
gentle + -**ly** = *gent**ly***
happy + -**ly** = *happ**ily***

B Complete the paragraph with the correct adverbs. Use the adjectives in parentheses and -*ly*.

I had an ¹_____ (extreme) weird dream last night. I was in a house, ²_____ (possible) my friends' house. ³_____ (sudden) a dinosaur ⁴_____ (random). appeared. It roared at me ⁵_____ (angry). Then I ⁶_____ (thankful) woke up. I'm not sure what the dream meant. It could mean nothing. Or, ⁷_____ (alternative) it means my friend is angry with me in real life.

Suffix -ive

Most words ending in -ive are adjectives. You can add the suffix -ive to some verbs to form adjectives. The suffix -ive means "having a certain quality."

VERB + -IVE = ADJECTIVE

act + -**ive** = act**ive**, meaning "busy doing things"

A Write the correct adjectives to complete the sentences.

active	alternative	creative	distinctive	productive

1. The design of the Eiffel Tower is _____ .

2. Having no distractions helps you be more _____ .

3. If you are busy a lot, you are _____ .

4. Someone who is artistic is usually _____ .

5. Compared to fossil fuels, solar power is a better .

Word families Nouns, verbs, and adjectives

You can add a suffix to some verbs to change them to nouns and adjectives.
Common suffixes for nouns are: -ation and -ion.
Common suffixes for adjectives are: -ed, -ing, and -ive.

Many verbs can use the same suffixes, but others can't. For example, we can add -ion to connect to make the noun connection. But we can't add -ion to expect. "Expection" is not a word.

Some words can be both nouns and verbs, and their spelling does not change.

VERB   NOUN

I **work** at a supermarket. It's hard **work**.

B Complete the chart with the correct noun and adjective forms. More than one answer may be possible. Use a dictionary to help you and to check your spelling.

Noun	Verb	Adjective
	act	
	create	
	organize	
	product	
	trouble	

Context clues

You can sometimes guess the meaning of unknown words using clues from the context. Sometimes the writer will restate something or give additional details. In other cases, the writer will give examples that help define the word.

Restatement: *I'm **excelling** in my tech class. <u>I got an "A" on the test!</u>*

Example: *E-books are **distracting**. For example, it's <u>easy to stop reading and click another app.</u>*

A Choose the correct definition of the words in bold. Use the context to help you guess the meaning. Then check your answers in a dictionary.

1. I am **proficient** at languages. For example, I can speak with my French, German, and Spanish colleagues.

   a. skillful   b. poor   c. fair

2. I **flunked** the test. In fact, my score was so bad I'll have to take the test again!

   a. did well   b. failed   c. missed

3. I've hit some **snags** with my essay. One snag is that my computer stopped working.

   a. questions   b. answers   c. problems

4. The snow has made the road **treacherous**. It was really hard to drive.

   a. busy   b. dangerous   c. cold

5. Getting a bad grade last year was an **anomaly**. Every other year I've had great grades.

   a. not normal   b. poor   c. normal event

Word families Nouns, verbs, and adjectives

Some words have noun, verb, and/or adjective forms.

   depression (noun)   *depress* (verb)   *depressing* (adjective)

Common suffixes for nouns are: *-ion*, *-ment*, and *-y*.

Common suffixes for adjectives are: *-ible*, *-ic*, *-ing*, and *-ive*.

Some words can be both nouns and verbs, and their spelling does not change.

VERB   NOUN

*I **work** at a supermarket. It's hard **work**.*

B Complete the chart with the correct forms of the words. Use a dictionary to help you and to check your spelling.

Noun	Verb	Adjective
	access	
		argumentative
		decisive
development		
	strategize	

VOCABULARY INDEX

*Academic words

VOCABULARY INDEX

SENTENCE TYPES

There are three types of sentences: simple, compound, and complex. These labels refer to how a sentence is organized, not how difficult the content is.

SIMPLE SENTENCES

Simple sentences contain a subject (s) and a verb (v). They have just one independent clause. An independent clause can stand alone.

    S   V

Bats are interesting animals.

    V   S   V

Do you like bats?

Simple sentences can contain more than one subject or verb.

    S   S   V

Bats and dolphins are mammals.

    S   V   V

Bats are nocturnal and have good night vision.

COMPOUND SENTENCES

Compound sentences contain at least two independent clauses (IC). These two clauses are combined with a connector called a *coordinating conjunction* (CC), such as *and, but, or, yet, so,* and *for.* Use a comma before the conjunction connecting two independent clauses.

       IC   CC   IC

Dogs are fun, **but** cats are easier to own.

         IC   CC   IC

Lea worked hard on the project, **so** she got a good grade.

COMPLEX SENTENCES

Complex sentences contain one independent clause (IC) and at least one dependent clause (DC). A dependent clause cannot stand alone. In some complex sentences, the dependent clause is an adverb clause. Adverb clauses begin with connectors called *subordinating conjunctions,* such as *while, although, because,* and *if.* Note that if a sentence begins with an independent clause, there is not a comma separating the two clauses. If a sentence begins with a dependent clause, there is a comma.

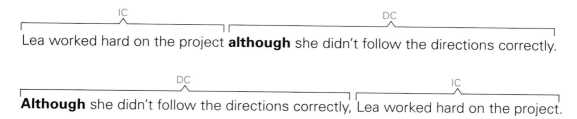

EDITING TIPS

Capitalize:

- ▶ the first word of every sentence.
- ▶ the pronoun *I.*
- ▶ people's titles, e.g., Ms., Mr., Mrs., Dr.
- ▶ proper names of people, places, and organizations.
- ▶ locations, e.g., street names, cities, states, countries, and rivers.
- ▶ days, months, and holidays.
- ▶ the names of languages and nationalities.

Punctuate:

- ▶ with a period (.) at the end of every sentence that is not a question.
- ▶ with a question mark (?) at the end of every sentence that is a question.
- ▶ with an exclamation mark (!) to show strong feelings. This is not used often in academic writing.
- ▶ with commas (,) to separate a list of three or more things and after some introductory words or phrases, e.g., *Hopefully, However, Finally,* and *Meanwhile,.*
- ▶ with a comma before combining words joining two sentences, e.g., *and, but, so,* and *or.*
- ▶ with an apostrophe (') to show possession.
- ▶ with quotation marks (" ") to show that you are using someone's exact words.

IRREGULAR VERB FORMS

Base form	Simple past	Past participle
be	was, were	been
beat	beat	beaten
become	became	become
begin	began	begun
bend	bent	bent
bite	bit	bitten
blow	blew	blown
break	broke	broken
bring	brought	brought
build	built	built
buy	bought	bought
catch	caught	caught
choose	chose	chosen
come	came	come
cost	cost	cost
cut	cut	cut
dig	dug	dug
dive	dived/dove	dived
do	did	done
draw	drew	drawn
drink	drank	drunk
drive	drove	driven
eat	ate	eaten
fall	fell	fallen
feed	fed	fed
feel	felt	felt
fight	fought	fought
find	found	found
fit	fit	fit/fitted
fly	flew	flown
forget	forgot	forgotten
forgive	forgave	forgiven
freeze	froze	frozen
get	got	got/gotten
give	gave	given
go	went	gone
grow	grew	grown
hang	hung	hung
have	had	had
hear	heard	heard
hide	hid	hidden
hit	hit	hit
hold	held	held
hurt	hurt	hurt
keep	kept	kept
know	knew	known

Base form	Simple past	Past participle
lay	laid	laid
lead	led	led
leave	left	left
lend	lent	lent
let	let	let
lie	lay	lain
light	lit/lighted	lit/lighted
lose	lost	lost
make	made	made
mean	meant	meant
meet	met	met
pay	paid	paid
prove	proved	proved/proven
put	put	put
quit	quit	quit
read	read	read
ride	rode	ridden
ring	rang	rung
rise	rose	risen
run	ran	run
say	said	said
sit	sat	sat
sleep	slept	slept
slide	slid	slid
speak	spoke	spoken
spend	spent	spent
spread	spread	spread
stand	stood	stood
steal	stole	stolen
stick	stuck	stuck
strike	struck	struck
swear	swore	sworn
sweep	swept	swept
swim	swam	swum
take	took	taken
teach	taught	taught
tear	tore	torn
tell	told	told
think	thought	thought
throw	threw	thrown
understand	understood	understood
upset	upset	upset
wake	woke	woken
wear	wore	worn
win	won	won
write	wrote	written

INDEX OF EXAM SKILLS & TASKS

Reflect is designed to provide practice for standardized exams, such as IELTS and TOEFL. This book has many activities that focus on and practice skills and question types that are needed for test success.

READING • Key Skills	IELTS	TOEFL	Page(s)
Evaluate ideas	X	X	78
Identify facts and opinions	X	X	134, 138
Make inferences	X	X	44, 48
Predict what you will read	X	X	6, 10, 24, 28, 42, 46, 60, 114, 136
Preview a text	X	X	64, 78, 82, 96, 100, 118, 132
Read or scan for specific details	X	X	8, 12, 26, 30, 44, 48, 62, 66, 78, 84, 98, 102, 116, 120, 134, 138
Read or skim for main ideas	X	X	8, 12, 25, 30, 44, 48, 60, 66, 78, 82, 96, 102, 114, 120, 132, 136
Understand charts and graphs	X		25, 29, 30,
Understand pronoun reference		X	80, 84
Understand the author's purpose		X	62

READING • Common Question Types	IELTS	TOEFL	Page(s)
Complete sentences, a summary, or a table	X		12, 25, 30, 48, 62, 84, 102, 116, 120, 132
Judge if details are true, false, or not given	X		12, 26, 78, 96, 138
Match information to a paragraph	X		8, 30, 48, 66, 78, 82, 136
Match information to categories		X	66, 98
Multiple choice or multiple response	X	X	44, 60, 114
Put information in order		X	98, 102
Short answer	X		8, 30, 102

WRITING • Key Skills	IELTS	TOEFL	Page(s)
Analyze graphs and charts	X		25, 29, 30, 67, 70, 71, 72, 77, 84
Brainstorm ideas	X	X	17, 23, 34, 52, 89, 107, 117, 125, 143
Describe a graph or chart	X		70, 72, 77
Give supporting ideas and details	X	X	50, 51, 53, 144
Organize a paragraph	X	X	13
Plan or outline what you will write	X	X	17, 36, 72, 90, 125
Review and edit to fix errors	X	X	16, 34, 52, 70, 71, 89, 106, 124, 143
Express supported opinions	X	X	4, 5, 66
Write a concluding paragraph	X	X	125, 140, 144
Write a paragraph	X	X	18, 36
Write an essay	X	X	104, 108, 126, 144
Write an introductory paragraph	X	X	122, 125, 144
Write concluding sentences	X	X	17, 36, 53, 90, 108
Write supporting sentences	X	X	14, 17, 36, 53, 86, 87, 90, 108, 125
Write topic sentences	X	X	14, 17, 32, 36, 53, 90, 108, 125

WRITING • Common Topics	IELTS	TOEFL	Page(s)
Communities and cultures	X	X	18, 36
Communication	X	X	36
Creativity	X	X	126
Learning	X	X	144
Entertainment	X	X	53
Travel	X	X	90
The future	X	X	108

CREDITS

Illustration: All illustrations are owned by © Cengage.

Cover © Dhafer Alshehri; **2–3** (spread) Peter Unger/The Image Bank Unreleased/Getty Images; **4** Bruce Dale/National Geographic Image Collection; **6–7** (spread) Richard Sharrocks/Moment/Getty Images; **10** Priscila Zambotto/Moment/Getty Images; **16** Kumar Sriskandan/Alamy Stock Photo; **18** Premium Stock Photography GmbH/Alamy Stock Photo; **20–21** (spread) Claudia Burlotti/The Image Bank/Getty Images; **22** © Crossing Borders Education; **24** Rob Stothard/Getty Images News/Getty Images; **26** James P. Blair/National Geographic Image Collection; **28** Glyn Kirk/AFP/Getty Images; **29** Courtesy of Glencairn Museum; **31** Hermes Images/AGF/Universal Images Group/Getty Images; **34** Lucy Lambriex/DigitalVision/Getty Images; **38–39** (spread) SuperStock/Alamy Stock Photo; **40** Really Easy Star/Alamy Stock Photo; **42–43** (spread) TCD/Alamy Stock Photo; **46–47** (spread) © Joel Sartore Photography; **49** Moviestore Collection Ltd/Alamy Stock Photo; **53** Kyodo News/Getty Images; **56–57** (spread) © Berndnaut Smilde; **58** Frederic Neema/laif/Redux; **60–61** (spread) © Valerie Ostenak; **64–65** (spread) © Pindar Van Arman/cloudpainter; **68** Wenn Rights Ltd/Alamy Stock Photo; **74–75** (spread) © Kristen Ryan; **76** National Geographic Image Collection; **78–79** (spread) © Lorraine Yip; **82–83** (spread) Tong Thi Viet Phuong/Moment/Getty Images; **85** AGE Fotostock/Alamy Stock Photo; **89** Westend61/Getty Images; **92-93** (spread) Travis P Ball/Getty Images Entertainment/Getty Images; **94** (t) NASA MSFC Earth Science Office, (cr) ITAR-TASS Photo Agency/Alamy Stock Photo; **96–97** (spread) Ben Horton/National Geographic Image Collection; **100–101** (spread) Courtesy of Google LLC; **103** Jim West/Alamy Stock Photo; **107** wunkley/Alamy Stock Photo; **110–111** (spread) Courtesy of Shantanu Suman, Courtesy of Aashim Tyagi, Courtesy of Shreedavy Babuji; **112** © Footage courtesy of SoulPancake, LLC; **114** primeimages/E+/Getty Images; **118–119** (spread) Tuul & Bruno Morandi/The Image Bank/Getty Images; **120** Gregory Kramer/DigitalVision/Getty Images; **124** Ami Vitale/National Geographic Image Collection; **126** Mike Segar/Reuters; **128–129** (spread) © Annie Griffiths; **130** Courtesy of François Schaer/Rolex Awards; **132–133** (spread) © Irlan Turhantoro; **136** Jeff Greenberg/Universal Images Group/Getty Images; **138** Jeff Greenberg/Universal Images Group/Getty Images; **142** VCG/Getty Images.